A TEXTBOOK OF MELODY

A Course in Functional Melodic Analysis

BY

DR. JOSEPH SMITS VAN WAESBERGHE
Professor at the Amsterdam Conservatory

Translated from the Dutch by
W. A. G. DOYLE-DAVIDSON

Senior Lecturer in English
Language and Literature in
the University of Leeds,
sometime
Professor of English in the
University of Nijmegen,
Holland

AMERICAN INSTITUTE OF MUSICOLOGY
1955

CONTENTS

PREFACE

The aim of this book is to attempt an analysis of melodic consciousness, to deduce the laws governing the formation of melodies, and to work out a method by which the application of these laws and the recognition of their use may be learnt.

It is by no means merely an arrangement for didactic purposes of existing books on melody — the number of these, anyhow, can be counted on the fingers[1]. In this very limited literature melody is regarded as consisting of three elements, rhythm, form and function, by the last of which is understood the mutual relationship between the different notes of a melody, a relationship which is defined according to the bass notes that support the melody or at least are latent in it. These bass notes, whether actually present or not, are at once both the foundation and the condensed summary of the harmonic development, and as such they give to the notes of the melody their place in the harmonic context, thus indicating their function.

The historian finds it difficult to accept this conception of melodic function. Although at first sight it might seem to suffice for an analysis of Western melodies of the polyphonic period, the historian finds himself faced by such an inexhaustible wealth of melodies of other periods and peoples whose harmonic consciousness can never thus be even satisfactorily indicated, let alone analysed, that he feels himself compelled to make a deeper search into the nature of melodic function. There are wonderful melodies which were never provided by the composers with a harmonic dress and which cannot, indeed, be harmonised satisfactorily according to the traditional rules of Western harmony; it would be to oversimplify — and moreover a very questionable procedure — to attempt to reduce their functions to the tonic, dominant and subdominant relationships which in the West were only discovered many centuries later and elsewhere have not been discovered yet. This is not to deny that modern harmony is an extension of a primary function inherent in musical sounds themselves, yet it would seem to be unjustified to try to explain melodic

---

[1] The best are W. Woehl, *Melodielehre* (Leipzig, 1923) and P. Goetschius, *Exercises in Melody-Writing* (New York, 1928); *cf.* P. Hindemith, *Unterweisung im Tonsatz* (*The Craft of Musical Composition*), Mainz 1937 (New York, 1941-43).

function entirely in terms of the harmonic, seeing that the former was known centuries before there was any question of harmonic consciousness. Note, moreover, that one melody can be harmonised in very different ways, while quite different melodies (involving different melodic functions) can be constructed over one harmonic foundation. The present method is therefore based on the conviction that melodic function is something quite independent and cannot be deduced completely from the harmonic context [2].

The method which is here set forth is intended for the use of professional teachers of music, music teachers in primary and secondary schools, of music psychologists and musicologists.

It may be asked whether it is desirable to devote any time to the teaching of melody in the professional training of musicians. This question I should prefer to answer by posing another: ought not a knowledge of the laws of harmony and counterpoint and the application of these to be preceded by a knowledge of the laws governing the formation of melodies and by some practice in writing and analysing melodies? [3]

Is it not by melody, after all, that music finally stands or falls? More and more music teachers, in fact, are gradually becoming convinced of the importance of the study of melody in professional training. Many, indeed, hold the view that such a study should be the foundation for the teaching of harmony.

To avoid misunderstanding, let it be observed that this would not mean any substantial increase in the theoretical work — first, because the theory of melody is a brief and straightforward business; second, because the study of melody is itself an introduction to harmony, making this subject easier in its early stages; third, because the study of melody can also simplify the teaching of other subjects, such as solfeggio and certain aspects of the history of music; fourthly, because an understanding of the theory of melody can be of great use in the practice of music; and finally, because a well-designed course in melody is much less a theoretical than a practical subject. This last consideration particularly is conclusive: the objections to including a course in melody as part of the professional training of musicians are few and are entirely outweighed by all the advantages that would result from it.

A course in melody in the sense envisaged above can also be regarded, for quite different reasons, as indispensable in the training

---

[2] It might be well worth while investigating to what extent the reverse is the case, namely, how far the laws of harmony can be deduced from the melodic functions.

[3] "Es ist erstaunlich, dass der Unterricht im Tonsatz bis heute keine Melodielehre kennt", P. Hindemith *op. cit.*, p. 199.

of music teachers in primary and secondary schools. In schools, indeed, we find a remarkable situation, for while on the one hand there is general agreement about the great importance of melodic improvisation, on the other hand very often little or no attention is actually paid to it. One reason for this, undoubtedly, is that there is no satisfactory textbook on the subject to help the teacher. Form and rhythm offer no difficulties, but as regards function the existing books on melody make the fundamental mistake of taking as their starting-point the major scale and of basing the rules of melodic function on the triad and the chord of the seventh. It may well be questioned whether it is wise with children to begin with the major scale. But quite apart from this, surely a method based on the laws of harmony is much too difficult for primary-school children — if not even for the teachers themselves. What these teachers need is a knowledge of the rules by which melodies can be constructed from different notes restricted in range (fourths, fifths, etc.) and of how to judge such melodies. It should be sufficient for music teachers in primary schools to be trained in the hearing, reproducing and judging of melodies, if need be without any training in harmony at all. What they need urgently, therefore, is a method based, not on rules deduced from harmony, but on those of the melodic tone-relationships.

The book here offered is a first attempt to satisfy this need. It begins, therefore, not with the major and minor scale, nor even with the ecclesiastical modes or pentatonic scales, but with the material presented by two successive notes, a group which is then gradually extended. Exercises based on these groups are worked out and observations made concerning the functional relations of the various notes of the group, and finally the resultant law is stated. For melodic training in the school it will be enough if the teacher knows and can apply these laws and in addition is familiar with one or two other melodic principles and with the chief types of melodic structure. He will then be able to teach musical improvisation in a series of progressive exercices, and he will also be able to judge and to correct the pupils' exercises.

As the principles of melodic form [4] (question and answer, structure of melodic phrases, song-form, etc.) are sufficiently explained in other books, and as good care is generally devoted to the methodical development of rhythmical aptitude, both musical and muscular, in children, these parts of the subject have here been relegated to the background. This was necessary because the book is intended also

[4] This method therefore constitutes no more than a foundation on which for each of the educational branches a complete course in melody and melodic style especially designed for, and based on the practice of each, can be worked out.

for the professional musician and the musicologist — and it is obvious that a method to suit these must be quite different from one designed for teachers in primary and secondary schools.

This book has also been written for psychologists and musicologists: for the former because a knowledge of the functional laws of melodically ordered tones will be useful in the designing of melodic tests; for the latter (and not least for experts in comparative musicology) because the scientific study of melodies and collections of melodies, of both past and present, here and in other parts of the world, and the analysis, both independent and comparative, of these is impossible without a knowledge of the fundamental laws of melody.

This book is therefore concerned with what is the most important part of the subject, melodic function. Hence it takes as its starting-point and as its most important activity just what is wanting altogether in existing books on melody. It is this lack which has been responsible for the teaching of melody being neglected, even though its importance in musical training has been called in question by none of the pundits. May this attempt, therefore, contribute to the restoration to favour of this important subject.

If I am justified in my expectation that musicologists and the best teachers of music will be interested in this subject, I should be grateful if they would let me know what alterations and additions they would be glad to see made in any subsequent editions of this book. I should like to take this opportunity of thanking my colleagues E. W. Mulder and B. Huijbers S.J. for all the help they have given me in this first attempt at designing a course in melody based on the functional affinities of the notes of a melody.

CHAPTER ONE

INTRODUCTION

§ 1. General Introduction

Young children pass through various stages of musical development, among which may be distinguished the perception of rhythm,
the observation and reproduction of rhythm in sound, and lastly the
expression of rhythm in sounds of various pitch. In general it may be
said that in childhood the ability develops to recognise groups of notes
(short phrases) as units. The conclusion follows that, exceptions apart,
children are naturally sensitive to melody. For what else but the very
essence of a melody is a structural unit of several notes of different
pitch? What *is* a melody, in the technical sense?

A melody consists of a number of notes of different pitch arranged
so as to constitute a unit as regards (external) form and movement
and according to the laws of the functional relations existing between
them.

This definition requires closer examination.

1. The making of a melody consists in the arranging to form a
whole of a variety of elements; that is, it is a "building", a "putting-
together". This is expressed in Latin by the verb *componere*, whence
is derived our word "to compose". In the Middle Ages melody-making
was regarded as the only true composing: a composer was called a
modulator, that is, a melody-maker, just as the Greeks had already
called the art of composition μελοποιία (melopoiía), "the construction
of melodies".

2. The material which is thus given form consists of "a number
of notes of different pitch". Consequently we cannot speak of melody
unless this material includes at least two notes of different pitch [1].

Seeing that it is a characteristic quality of music to give rise to
related variations and seeing that the possibilities of variation offered
by two different notes are limited in the extreme, little in the way

---

[1] With a single note one can make a quite satisfactory *rhythmical* statement but not a
musical one.

of melody can be expected from such restricted material. Let it be stated at once, therefore, that we cannot speak of melody in any true sense unless we have at our disposal at least three different notes.

3. By "(external) form" is meant the structure of a melody in its various parts, such as arsis and thesis, opening and closing sections, question and answer, and the melodic relationships between the parts, as these are indicated by letters, e.g. *a-b*, *a-c*.

4. Next, a melody must be arranged according to its "movement". This can be either a free rhythm, or rhythm bound to measure, or measure alone.

The last needs no explaining: measure is a constantly recurring alternation of heavy and light periods. The second, rhythm and measure, requires the grouping of units of measure (bars) in larger units of tension and relief. Just as in verse there is a basic measure, and yet often it only springs to life when in delivery the verse-feet are grouped together in new units of tension and relief, so also in music there is very often a similar life-giving movement extending beyond the limit of the bar. A piece of music, though noted in bars, has thus in performance a living rhythm of its own and is not just played mechanically in strict time.

For the first, free rhythm, a comparison may also be made with poetry in so far as "free verse" exists, verse, that is, which is not bound to a prescribed number of feet but in which the accents — whether fixed in number or not — give rise to a movement in which there are points of tension and relief. So also in music which is independent of measure the accents (whether related to word-stresses or not) give rise to a movement, a free rhythm (as in plainsong).

5. There has already been mention in the Preface of the "functional relations or affinities between notes" in the sense of the special functional relationships existing between the notes of a melody, which is not the same thing as the harmonic relationship that can be derived from it.

These relations or affinities can be of various kinds. In anticipation of what will be established by experiment in the following pages a brief summary may here be given of the different sorts of tonal affinity that may occur in a melody. They can be divided into four main groups: a. functional identity; b. functional linking; c. functional unit; and d. contrast.

a. *Functional identity* is present (leaving out of account for the moment the influence of rhythm and form) when a note is followed immediately by another of the same pitch, and also in the case of certain ornaments.

b. *Functional linking* arises through the presence of transitional notes, e.g. *so* between *fa* and *la*. Both of these relationships lack the variety which is needed to give a melody life. This is imparted by the two following functions.

c. *Functional unit*, by which is meant the unit formed by two notes (e.g. *fa* and *la*) the tonal relationship between which is such that the one is attracted towards the other (*fa* to *la*) not by reason of any opposition between them but on account of this relationship, so that when the second note has been reached a tension is set up which is relaxed on a return to the first note (*la* to *fa*). This concept will be explained in more detail later.

d. *Functional contrast* represents an absolute functional opposition and is produced by *other* notes than those which constitute a functional unit.

All that it is important to know at the moment is that the functions which the notes of a melody (melodically considered) mutually possess are of four main kinds each having a different degree of variation; in other words, the affinities between the notes of a melody fall into four main groups. It should be noted that the functional affinity of a note is not determined exclusively by its relation to the immediately preceding or following note (or to both), but can extend to a group or groups of preceding and succeeding notes. Note also that rhythm and structure can also exert a determining influence on the nature of this affinity.

To sum up what has been said so far, it may be stated generally that we are sensitive to melody as an ordered whole consisting of a number of notes on different degrees of the scale. It is the business of a textbook on melody to make us *conscious* of the laws and rules in accordance with which this ordering of the notes of a melody is carried out, and its aim is accordingly twofold: on the one hand to enable us to analyse, judge and if necessary correct existing melodies, and on the other to help us to write good, musically justified melodies. In the Preface it has already been stated and the reasons therefor given that in this book attention will be devoted particularly to these laws of the functional affinities of the notes of a melody.

§ 2. Some details concerning the present method

It is desirable to introduce this method with some remarks of a practical nature.

1. What modal relation has the material chosen here as point of departure?

A method of melodic analysis must start with some material or other. In this case it might be a major scale, the ecclesiastical modes, the pentatonic scale, the twelve-note system, etc.

Here, however, as has been said in the Preface, the starting-point will be notes having no modal connection. Although in a group of notes it is always possible to see a connection with some scale (a connection which is often quite subjective), the reader is advised not to seek any such connection at first. He may rest assured that sufficient attention will be paid to scales at a later stage.

To begin with, two and then three successive notes will be taken, chosen arbitrarily from the diatonic scale, not in order to exclude the twelve-note scale but only because a start must be made somewhere and for pedagogic reasons this choice is the most convenient. The twelve-note or chromatic scale will be discussed in its place, in as far at least as a group of notes from this series will be selected as independent notes in a melody (and not as fortuitous ornaments or chromatic alterations).

2. Notation

It has been a problem to know how best to indicate the notes of the diatonic scale. For referring to relative pitch the tonic solfa notation can be used. But tonic solfa has one drawback, it does not distinguish notes beyond the range of a single octave. Numbers are less suitable for our purpose in as far as the figure 1, for example, is too closely associated with a particular degree of the scale, an indication which is not conveyed by the letters C-D-E-F-G used to represent absolute pitch. The fact that the first note of the major scale is C and not A, is not found in teaching practice to offer any particular difficulty.

For the representation in the text of pitch and of portions of melodies the mediaeval notation by letters has been chosen, in as far as these were also used in the Middle Ages to represent *relative* pitch (the tonic solfa was a hexachord system and did not become an octave system until the fifteenth century, after the Middle Ages were over). This letter-system obviates the objections just mentioned, as long as it is remembered that the letters have values which are just as relative as those which the tonic solfa syllables have now. This series is as follows:

A B C D E F G a b c d e f g aa (or a'), etc.

14

In our quotations these letters have thus the same relative meaning as La-Ti-Do-Re-Mi-Fa-Sol-La-Ti-Do-Re-Mi-Fa-Sol-La, etc. (or Lah-Te-Doh-Rah-Me-Fah-Soh-Lah-Te-Doh-Rah-Me-Fah-Soh-Lah).

3. Principal Notes

It was stated in § 5 of the General Introduction that the functional relations obtaining between the notes of a melody exhibit different degrees of variation. The notes with functional identity and linking offer little or no variation. On the other hand, all the life in melody depends entirely on the relations of the functional unit and of contrast. It is these two functional relations which give to the notes concerned their outstanding importance in a melody; these notes will be called the principal notes of a melody. The meaning of this term can also be indicated negatively: the principal notes of a melody are those which have no unimportant functions such as functional repetition or linking. Just as in the harmonic analysis of a composition in parts only the special functions are indicated, so also the course of a melody according to the functional relations of its notes can be represented *by writing out the principal notes*, omitting, that is to say, those which have no function (repetitions and ornaments) and those which have linking function (transitional notes). Such a representation is very useful in analysing a melody or in making a comparative analysis of several melodies. Naturally also, just as in harmonic analysis, this summary of the functions can be further reduced to an outline of the more or most important of these. This is also applicable to a melody, although it only has theoretical interest. The more summary such an analysis becomes, the further removed it is from the actual living melody itself and its aesthetic qualities.

4. Tonic, Dominant, Fundamental Note and Central Note

If European music since the early Middle Ages is viewed from the standpoint of tonic and dominant, it is seen that not always the same meaning attaches to these terms: in the various modal scales the dominant, for example, reckoned from the tonic, can be either a major or a minor third, a fourth, a fifth, or a minor sixth. To avoid misunderstanding, therefore, the terms tonic and dominant will for the time being not be used.

If they are employed — and this will only be in connection with harmony — they will have the meaning which they usually have in harmony. As far as melody is concerned the term to be used instead of tonic will be *fundamental note*, a term which is not used in harmony and yet is perfectly clear. Related to this is the term *central note*, which will be used when in a melody, while the fundamental note remains the same, a note on another degree of the scale becomes temporarily

15

the melodic centre. For example, if we have an opening *so-la-so*, where *so* is the fundamental note, followed by the recitation of several syllables on the fourth, *do*, above, then *do* becomes temporarily a new point of departure, a displaced tonal centre.

Where music in the old ecclesiastical modes is in question, then to avoid misunderstanding the terms dominant and mediant (which in this music have a special meaning) will be replaced by *dominans* (plural *dominantes*) and *medians* (plural *mediantes*).

5. Recitation technique and melodic technique

The process involved in the composition of a melody (in the technical sense defined in the General Introduction) is called *melodic technique*. There is also a *recitation technique*. There exists a distinct recitation (or chant) form, occurring, for example, in psalmody (to be distinguished from the recitative of opera or oratorio, although there may be similarities between them). This form is not melody in the strict sense of the word, in that its most important melodic characteristic is the repetition of several syllables on a single note, and in that the element of movement is of little importance. As a result this technique differs from that of melody and it is therefore convenient to distinguish the two. In this course recitation technique will be dealt with first in its simplest form, without either rising introduction (intonation, *initium*) or descending cadence (ending, *terminatio* or *finalis*).

6. The exercises

A textbook on melody is not a reading-book but a book of *exercises*, intended, like a book on harmony, to be used under the guidance of a teacher. This book has therefore been planned in such a way that the laws governing tonal relationships are one by one both deduced and then applied in exercises based on specified material. The student should not go outside or beyond these exercises. In doing them the following points should be kept in mind:

a. Account must be taken of the musical sensibility and powers of expression, as well as of the extent to which these have been developed, of those who are doing the exercises. As the formative elements in a melody are three in number — the melodically functional affinities of the notes, the form, and the rhythm or measure (or both) — the teacher should be careful to see that the exercises to be done are adjusted to the capabilities of the pupil in regard to these three elements.

It may be that the pupil has a musical aptitude and has achieved a standard of musical education that will enable him to write a melody in accordance with the exercise in which all three of these elements are taken satisfactorily into account.

But it may also happen that a pupil succeeds in doing the exercise as far as the laws of functional affinity are concerned and yet fails to arrange the notes properly within the framework of a measure. In such a case the teacher must go to work progressively, in each of the exercises requiring at first only the most important element — a succession of notes without rhythm, say, but satisfying the laws of affinity. Attention to form — arrangement in opening and closing sections, etc. — would then be a second stage that will offer few difficulties. But the teacher will have to devote special attention to the technical training of the pupil in the moulding of the melodic material into a definite rhythm. There are various ways of doing this. One can start by passing from a free rhythm to a fixed rhythm, by putting bar-lines in a melody dictated without rhythm — and so on. My experience is that the best results can be obtained by a method involving a motor reaction. The teacher sings a phrase having considerable motor tension (suited, of course, to the character of the pupil) — one, that is, which arouses a lively desire to continue or complete it [1]. The pupil has then to repeat this phrase himself; his musical feeling and imagination will be aroused and he will try to develop this melodic opening into a complete melody.

This method has the advantage of revealing to the pupil through his own experience that music-making (in this preliminary stage) is above all an expression of pleasure; that it is a consequence of musical motor tension; and that the composing of melodies can be aided by such prepared motor conditioning and not least by such rhythmically lively phrases discovered by himself. A method of this sort can be extended to cover a complete rhythmical training.

The teacher would first give the whole opening section of a melody and ask the pupil to complete it; at the next stage he would give only a complete phrase, and finally only an important opening figure (arsis or thesis). It is important to add here that the further a melody progresses the fewer become the possible ways of finishing it and the more difficult therefore it becomes to finish it (except, of course, for the closing formula).

An example may make this clear. Suppose the exercise is to compose a melody out of the notes *do-re-mi-fa-sol-la*, with *do* as fundamental note. If in the example given below only the upbeat and the first full bar are sung, with lively motor tension, then the possible ways of completing the melody are numerous. But *every note added further* reduces the possibilities. The last two bars, containing four or five notes, have been omitted deliberately, to show that, when

[1] With professional pupils the teacher need only give a rhythmical phrase, without any melody.

so much has been given, the musical statement (that is, the expression of the musical thought) has been already carried so far that, in a manner of speaking, only a full stop still remains to be added.

It is obvious, of course, that a musical statement such as the above can be made in a variety of ways, with all sorts of melodic and rhythmical ornaments and unessential variations. To return to our starting-point, namely that in the working of the exercises the pupils' capabilities must be taken into account, in what follows here complete freedom is left to the teacher in this respect. Moreover, since this book is concerned principally with the functional relationships, the examples quoted have been deliberately chosen so as to avoid all complexities of time and rhythm. The teacher is advised emphatically not to underestimate the importance of the training of the pupils' motor reactions (how many rhythmless organ improvisations regularly offend our ears!) and to require from them melodic exercises in more lively rhythms than, for the reasons just given, are to be found in the examples in this book.

b. One of the sections of this book (page 70) deals with the interval of the fourth. It is desirable that the use of the fourth in melodic exercises should as far as possible, that is to say, as long as melodic improvisation is not checked thereby, be avoided until that section has been reached. In analysing examples of melodies let the teacher avoid discussing the fourth until the chapter dealing with it has been worked through.

c. It will be noticed that the exercises in this text often include a further limitation of the material selected to illustrate the functional relationships. For example, there may be mention of an upper second as prosodic note while the exercise deals only with a major and not a minor second. This has been done deliberately. When the chapter on euphony is reached it will become clear to the pupil why the practical exercises were for the time being limited to the major second although the relevant law refers to the second in general: this last is correct but with a restriction which is dealt with in the chapter just mentioned. After the exercises given have been done, then, still taking account of what has just been said, they can be done again with

18

other notes, though avoiding for the time being *do* and *fa* as funda-mental notes.

7. Melody, not harmony

For readers who have studied harmony it will require no little effort to consider a melody from a purely melodic, not harmonic, point of view. Only as we proceed will it become clear how important it is to listen to a melody from the standpoint of the functional relations of its notes and for the time being to ignore its harmonic potentialities. Although these two aspects and the reasons for and consequences of distinguishing between them will be discussed later, let it be emphasised at once in the strongest terms that from the very beginning one should train oneself in purely melodic listening.

8. Exploring the world of sound

As some people like to introduce the study of melody by some consideration of the phenomena of sound in general, the following is suggested as a brief series of preliminary observations.

a. Given silence broken by a sound, say a shout.
Observation: sound attracts special attention.

b. Given silence broken by a sung note.
Observation: a sung note attracts attention more readily than what is spoken; psychologically it is a more special sort of utterance and hence it attracts greater attention than the spoken word.

c. Compare a spoken sentence with a recited (i.e. chanted) sentence.

d. Practical exercises in reciting (chanting) on a single note result in the observation of the following phenomena:

1. Dynamics: loud and soft word-groups; crescendo and de-crescendo.

2. Accentuation (by means of dynamics and phrasing); occur-rence in reciting of the phraseological accent (i.e. the normal sen-tence stress) and of the emphatic accent (an emotional accent of one sort or another). Recite a text phraseologically, making all syllables of equal length. (Note how sensitive the ear is in picking up every nuance in the recitation).

3. Movement: practice and observation of different speeds (slower, slow, fast, faster); prepared and unprepared cessation of the movement. Practice in reciting lines of verse and prose sentences in rhythm and tempo (together with 1 and 2 above).

Note 1. The transition to melodic accentuation in reciting will be dealt with in the following section.

Note 2. It is possible that in making the above-mentioned ob-servations or those of the immediately following sections, the pupil

19

may not understand what is being aimed at or its relation to the whole, in which case he will probably condemn the exercises as childish. If this seems likely to happen, or actually occurs, then it is the business of the teacher to make clear to the pupil that as it is a matter here of getting a methodical ear-training in the functional affinities of notes, it is necessary to develop one's ability to think about auditory musical impressions and to analyse one's auditory observations, and also that the exercises designed to aid this yield the best results if all unnecessary complications are avoided.

CHAPTER TWO

THE LAWS OF TONAL AFFINITY

§ 1. The functional affinities of two given notes

Note. It was remarked on page 12 that where there are only two notes one can hardly speak of melody in any true sense. The reasons for this will become clear as we proceed: a melody requires particular tonal tensions and contrasts which are only partially obtainable within the range of a second.

A. Recitation technique

1. *Given.* A reciting-tone with the second *above* it as an accentuation tone.

Exercise. Reciting-tone *a*, accentuation-tone *b*.

Note. When words are being set confusion must be avoided with regard to the choice of the syllable with the accentuation-tone. It is better for the exercise to be entirely musical, without words; if a text is taken then it is recommended that it should have some *general* content, e.g. a chorale or Latin text.

Observation. A recitation interrupted by a higher accentuation-tone (the two given tones being the only tonal material) requires normally a return to the reciting-tone. This is particularly noticeable if in the example given above one breaks off suddenly on the accentuation-tone, e.g. of *pó-puli* (better not on *gén-tes,* as in this case the function of the melodic half-close comes into the question).

The ear, hearing a fundamental note as reciting-tone and then becoming aware of a *raised* melodic accent, expects a return, as to a melodic point of repose, to the starting-point, the fundamental note.

21

B. Melodic technique

Given. A melody consisting of two notes a second apart.

Exercise. A melody on the notes G and a.

Observation. In a melody consisting of two notes a second apart one generally cannot be certain which of the two is the fundamental note. This is one of the reasons why no melody in the true sense can be constructed out of this limited material. For the same reason no law regarding their fundamental relation can be formulated.

Generally speaking, it can be said that with a melody of two notes a second apart the ear usually gives preference to the lower as the fundamental note, because the fundamental note has the function of being the point of repose of the melody and a lower note gives rise to less tension than a higher note (and consequently is the sooner felt to be the melodic point of repose, i.e. the fundamental note). This is illustrated by the sing-song heard when children are learning to add or multiply in class:

Six times six are thir - ty six

For the same reason it is very difficult to write melodies covering a range of a fourth or a fifth with the fundamental note on the fourth and fifth degrees respectively (the lowest note is called the first degree, and so on). We shall return to this later.

Terminology. In the recitation technique we met with an accent on the second above or below the reciting-tone. The same function occurs in the melodic technique, namely the momentary abandonment of a dominating note (in recitation this is the reciting-tone) by a transition to the second above or below it, thereby melodically ornamenting or stressing the dominating note — e.g. the ornamentation or accentuation of *la* by the notes *so* and *ti* in the following group (in three-four time): *la-so | la-ti | la-so | la* [1].

---

[1] A dash indicates that the preceding note is held for a second beat, while the diagonals represent the bar-lines.

22

If for this melodic accentuation the term "accented note" were to be used, this would give rise to misunderstanding, especially in melodic technique. For the word "accent" immediately suggests a dynamic or rhythmical accentuation. Here, however, we are concerned solely with a melodic accent which can occur at rhythmically unimportant as well as at important points; that is, either on a light or a heavy beat of the bar, on a syllable which is either stressed or unstressed. In melodic technique, therefore, the term "accented note" is better avoided.

Seeing that the speech-accent of Greek was melodic, this melodic accented note can appropriately be given the Greek name for accent, προσῳδία (prosodía), and can be called a *prosodic note*.

§ 2. The functional affinities of three given notes

A. Recitation technique

1. *Given.* A recitation interrupted by accentuation on a lower second followed by an upper second and then returning to the reciting tone.

Exercise. Reciting-tone *a*, with accentuation of two successive syllables on G and *b*.

Observation. (The following observation can be made particularly clear by breaking off on the upper accented note *b* and then asking how the recitation must be completed): If a recited fundamental note is heard, interrupted by an upper second followed by a lower second, then

1. these two new notes form a contrast with the fundamental note;
2. they constitute a unit over against the fundamental note;
3. after them the ear demands a return to the fundamental note.
The necessity for this return is felt much more strongly here than in the case of only two notes (see § 1 above).

Law. Over against a recited fundamental note the upper and lower second form a contrasting third which, once it has been heard, demands a return to the reciting-tone.

2. *Given.* A recitation with a melodic accentuation rising to the

23

second and third above, followed by a return in the same or a different order.

Exercise. Reciting-tone G, with prosodic notes *a* and *b*.

Introductory examples. If the following is sung:

and the function of the third, *G-b*, is compared with that of the second, *a*, then it is observed that between the notes of the third there exists a relationship to which the second (*a*) forms a contrast. The mere hearing of this contrasting note prepares the way for G, confirming it as the fundamental note. This succession of notes therefore forms a complete concluding whole. If with this is compared the following:

then it is observed that the second conclusion is by no means so complete. This becomes even clearer when the two formulae are juxtaposed in succession:

The last section constitutes a complete, definitive ending. So much by way of preparation; here is an example of the exercise:

Observation. The third above the reciting-tone has a family relationship with the fundamental note, while the upper second forms a contrast with it. It being of the essence of a cadence to confirm the fundamental note (preferably by means of its contrasting note), it is better in an exercise such as this to use for the cadence an accented

24

second rather than an accented third, as the third-relationship offers no contrast with the fundamental note.

Note. If the two following examples are compared, a change of function will be observed on the second degree (*a*):

In the first case it is merely transitional; this is called functional linking. In the second case the word-accentuation produces a contrast with the fundamental note of the kind just mentioned. Whether a second between two notes, a third apart, has contrasting or linking function depends on whether, as a result of its rhythmical placing or its relation (especially in recitation) to the word-accent, it is stressed or not [2].

Law. The relationship in recitation technique between the fundamental note and the second and third above it is different in the two cases: with the third it has a family relationship; to the second it presents a contrast. For this reason, when there are thirds, a conclusion with the upper second immediately preceding the fundamental note (unless it is merely transitional) is stronger and more effective than one with the upper third.

An unaccented second between two notes a third apart has the function of linking these two degrees.

Note. The same result is obtained with a recitation having the same melodic accentuation but with a second and a third (a major second and a major third) *below* the reciting-tone.

It will be noted that a fundamental note with an accentuation-tone [3] on the *major* third (in contrast with the *minor* third) below gives the impression of being forced, — starting, e.g., with *F* or *c* as fundamental note and descending to *E-D* or *b-a*. The reason for this effect of being forced lies in the fact that in the recitation as we have had it so far (without intonation or ending) it is unnatural,

---

[2] A similar phenomenon is observable in the harmonic functions.

[3] "Accentuation-tone" (not "prosodic note") is used here deliberately, for in recitation technique a melodic accent can occur on a second, a third, and even, if desired, on a fourth; whereas in melodic technique the normal interval for the accent is the second, and it is this accented second which is termed the prosodic note.

when there are three notes together covering a major third, for the highest of them to be the fundamental note; the fundamental note has the function of being the melodic point of repose, calling therefore for a minimum of exertion or tension — so that in this case the highest note, being the one requiring the greatest exertion, naturally sounds forced as the fundamental note.

With the minor third, however, the situation is different, as will be explained later in the section on the principles of vocal euphony.

B. Melodic Technique

1. *Given.* A melody formed from three notes covering a major third, with the middle one as fundamental note.

Exercise. To compose such a melody with the notes G - a - b, a being the fundamental note.

Observation. If a melody is constructed out of three notes together covering a major third, the middle note being the fundamental note, then the upper and lower seconds can be heard either separately or as having a mutual relationship. If they occur separately, then each is a prosodic note of the fundamental note (see Ex. 12, beginning, or altered as follows: a-Ga | a-a- | G-a- | a-); if they occur together, then they form a third which contrasts as a unit with the fundamental note, a unit which functionally requires a return to the fundamental note (see Ex. 12, bars 2-4 : a- | b-G- | a).

Law. In a melody of three successive notes covering a major third and with the middle note as fundamental note, the ear is aware of the *combination* of the lowest with the highest in a contrasting unit functionally calling for a return to the fundamental note; the highest and lowest notes, each occurring *separately* before and after the fundamental note, have the function of acting as melodic accents of the fundamental note, on the one hand constituting a tonal contrast

26

calling for the fundamental note, on the other serving to confirm the fundamental note.

Note 1. In the recitation technique of § 1 we encountered the upper and lower seconds of the reciting-tone as prosodic notes functioning as tonal variants, departures from the principal note requiring a return to it. We saw that the same function can also occur in a melody. If, however, this accentuation comes on a rhythmically unimportant part of the beat, as e.g. in:

then the function of the accentuation, in the sense of a contrast with the principal note, is much weaker; the prosodic note is in this case not much more than an ornamentation of the principal note. As thus the contrasting function of the prosodic note can, by placing it in a rhythmically unimportant position, be weakened to a mere tonal variation (one which in writing out the principal notes of a melody has to be omitted), so likewise for the same reason the contrasting function of the third (the upper and the lower seconds of the fundamental note) can be weakened to a mere ornamental figure — e.g.:

This weakening by no means eliminates the contrast completely: after *a-Gb* or *a-bG* the ear still expects a return to *a*.

Note 2. With the melodic material limited to three notes it is not easy to compose a melody having the middle note as fundamental note. The reason for this is that the number of functional variations is very restricted; only two prosodic notes (the upper and lower second) are available, with the contrast between these two together and the fundamental note — this last is called the contrasting third of a note. It will be seen later that the greatest number of functional contrasts is to be obtained with the material contained in two out of the four principal Gregorian modes, namely the Dorian and the Mixolydian. From this it follows that it is easier to compose a melody in one of these two modes than in the major or minor scale, in which the number of possible variations is considerably smaller.

On account of the limited number of functional variants possible it is recommended in general in composing melodies covering a third that the melody should begin with the fundamental note. If this is not done, there is likely to be considerable uncertainty as to which *is* the fundamental note. A striking but entirely justified example of such temporary uncertainty is provided by the following scheme of a children's song that occurs in many versions:

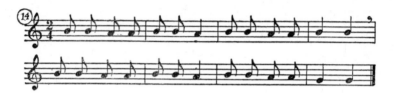

(also occurring with *b-b* in the last bar)

How is this melody to be analysed? Clever use is here made of the circumstance that with only two notes a second apart the identification of the fundamental note presents difficulties. Here it seems that we have an interplay between the two notes *b* and *a* of such a kind that until the last bar but one we do not know which of the two is the fundamental note. Then in the bar before the last *a* turns out to be a preparatory step to the note G, which has not yet been heard. Melodically this is a joke: neither *a* nor *b* makes any attempt to secure for itself the function of fundamental note (though this does happen if the melody ends on *a* or *b*); the note *b*, which at the beginning seems to be the most important note, turns out eventually to be the upper third of the fundamental note G. This upper third alternates with the second below it; at last the fundamental note is heard and with that the fun is over. The melodic course of this musical game has the closest possible correspondence with the children's game that accompanies it.

Generally speaking, it will be noted over and over again in children's songs that the melody does not end on the fundamental note or tonic but on the third or fifth above. This phenomenon and that which we have already mentioned of the fundamental note only being heard for the first time at the end of a tune is to be explained by the fact that a song is for children a free and unrestricted playing with notes in which there is indeed a definite form but one not so constructed as to obey all the rules of form imposed by the psychological make-up of adults.

The phenomenon of the condensed musical form of the child (compare the spontaneous songs of children and note how concise they are) might perhaps be compared with the child's expression of

28

emotion and thought, in which few words are used to express what should be said in many more words in a complete sentence.

Note 3. The contrasting third of which mention has been made above has the same function in its minor form in the position *F/GE/F* (*c/db/c*) but is weaker in the position *E/FD/E* (*b/ca/b*). The reason for this will be given later in the chapter on the principles of euphony. It is therefore better to postpone the writing of melodies covering a minor third and with *E* or *b* as fundamental note.

2. *Given.* A melody formed from three notes covering a major third, with the lowest note as fundamental note.

Exercise. To compose such a melody with the notes *G-a-b*, *G* being the fundamental note,

First example:

Observation. The repeated fall of a third in the first bar has the character of a unit; the two notes of the third are like two balancing poles whose alternation is interrupted by an extraneous third note *a*. The alternation of *b* and *G* is brought to a temporary rest on *a*. In the next two bars *a* is first given emphasis as the important opening note by means of the lower second, thus: *a-G-a*. When now, after this stress on *a*, the principal third is heard (*a-b/G- -*), one feels that a resolution on *a* is needed. Thus in the first four bars we have: *b-G-b-a a-b-G-a.*

Bars 5 and 6 are an extension of the *G-b-G* formula, in that *a* appears first in linking function between *G* and *b*, next as a contrasting second of *b* on a rhythmically unimportant beat (thereby increasing the importance of *b*) and finally as a transitional note (a functional link) back to *G*.

The third *G-/a-/b* with wich the last two bars begin again demands a progression to *a*; now that our feeling for form tells us that the melody is approaching its end, a good cadence requires a strong emphasis on the counter-note *a* over against the fundamental note *G*. This is why the *a* can, indeed must, for a time dominate the final stages of the melody (*b* is a prosodic note of *a* and thus further establishes its prominence), yet it must at last yield the supremacy to the fundamental note. We note, then, that *b-G* together form a

29

unit which we call a *third-unit;* between the two notes of this third
there is a certain tension (represented in this example by their
balancing alternation), and this is termed *the functional unit of the third.*
In relation to this third as a functional unit the intermediate degree *a*
constitutes a contrast; therefore (unless *a* is a transitional note) we
call it the *counter-note* of the third.

Expressed in terms of its principal notes this melody appears as
follows:

Note. In writing out the principal notes of a melody there is usually
no need to put the bar-lines, except, as here, for the sake of clarity.

Second example:

Observation. The beginning of this example is the same as that of the
preceding. This time, however, the alternation of *b* and *G* is not interrupted by the counter-note *a* but, with *a* as a transitional note to *G*,
comes to rest naturally on the fundamental note; the latter is, so to
speak, heavier on the see-saw than its companion. We have now
heard the functional unit of the third on the fundamental note but
music demands variety and so, if the result is to be a living melody,
the counter-note *a* must be given the greatest prominence in the
next section.

This is achieved by the threefold repetition of *a* on the first,
fourth and first beats of the next two bars. But the end must not
be reached yet, so the last *a* does not descend to the fundamental
note but seeks the note to which it bears the same functional relation,
namely the upper third *b*; expressed in metaphor, for the moment
the upper third dominates the see-saw of the principal thirds, and
the heavier fundamental note is left in the air — so that the game
is not yet over. What, expressed in principal notes, we have heard
so far is: *b-G-b-G-a-a-b.*

In the fifth and sixth bars the intermediate note *a* is first a transitional note to *G,* then a prosodic note of *G,* and then again a tran-

30

sitional note to *b*. The statement accordingly consists of *b-G-G-b*, the concluding of which on *b* is again an indication that the end has not yet been reached. This ending will have to give prominence to the counter-note *a* for two reasons: (1) as a functional contrast in the cadence; (2) by way of contrast to the preceding third section on the principal third [4]. This is achieved in the present example by the progression *a-b a-a* (where *b* is the prosodic note). The repetition of the fundamental note then brings the whole thing to a definitive conclusion.

Reduced to its principal notes the whole melody is therefore as follows:

It will be noted that the reduction of a good melody results in a succession of notes which is itself a melody, albeit without rhythm; that is to say, it has melodic potentialities although it is not itself a living melody.

Law. In a melody of three notes covering a major third and with the lowest note as fundamental note, the relationship between the latter and the third above is felt by the ear to be one of tension between two related notes, which thus constitute a unit to which the intermediate note (unless it is merely transitional) forms a contrast.

This tension between the lowest or fundamental note and the third above it is not enough to provide the only tonal variation in a melody; a desirable further variation is supplied by the occurrence of the middle note as a counter-note. Moreover, use can also be made of the principle of tonal accentuation.

Note 1. If one is required to construct a melody out of two successive major seconds one must ask oneself first which of the three notes is to be the fundamental note. For the reasons already given on pages 22 and 25 the highest note is practically speaking not eligible [5].

If the fundamental note comes on the lowest degree, then it forms a functional unit with the third above, with which — and this is the most important functional contrast — the middle note constitutes a contrast.

If the fundamental note is on the second degree, then the most

---

[4] The seventh bar may also be read *a-b-b-a*, resulting in a principal-third cadence, *cf.* p. 75.

[5] This is not to say that it is impossible to compose melodies with this note as the fundamental note, but if this attempted, then the law given on page 25 applies (see also the note on the same page).

important functional contrast is the linking of the seconds above and below the fundamental note to form a contrasting third that demands resolution on the fundamental note. In both cases the prosodic note provides a further functional variation, though a weaker one.

Moreover the second degree can occur as a transitional note from the first to the third degree and *vice versa*, in which case it has only a linking function. In this last case only the principal notes are prominent. What has been said in this paragraph is merely a repetition of the laws given on pages 26 and 31.

Note 2. If the function of the lower prosodic note (a major second) is compared with that of the upper prosodic note, then it will be observed that in general — apart from a particular melodic progression in a cadence — the lower second accentuates the fundamental note (e.g. *a-G-a*, where *a* is the fundamental note) more clearly than the upper second (*a-b-a*).

One might say that the lower second rather than the upper second has the function of confirming the fundamental note. Compare *a-G-b-a* with *a-b-G-a* and ask yourself which of the two groups makes the more definitive conclusion.

Note 3. Experience shows that younger children easily go out of tune when learning melodies covering a third which are new to them. On the other hand it is a remarkable fact that this generally does not happen when they are singing well-known children's songs. Attention is drawn to this phenomenon only for the sake of teachers who may be concerned.

Going out of tune on thirds and especially on two ascending major seconds is for the rest a phenomenon that does not appear only in children's singing!

Note 4. Below is given a melody of the Weddas of Ceylon, a dwarf people whose cultural development is very low. The *c* has only prosodic function in relation to the *b*, as a result of which the melodic interplay between the fundamental note *a* and its upper second *b* achieves a variety which imparts to this succession of notes with its rhythm and simple repetition of phrase a definitely melodic character [6].

---

[6] A great many melodies recovered for us by comparative musicologists can only be reproduced approximately in our notation. In applying to them the laws of melody this fact must be taken into account. Yet it will be noted that these laws can be applied to this music, and the reason is that from this point of view it does not make any difference if a second or a third in this music differs by a few vibrations from the corresponding intervals we use.

§ 3. The functional affinities of four given notes

Note. Recitation technique, as we have had it in the preceding sections (i.e., without *initium* and *terminatio*) is less practicable with four notes and more. It will be omitted, therefore, here and in the sections to follow. But *psalmodic* recitative with four and more notes will still be treated separately.

Only melodic technique, therefore, will be considered in this and the immediately following sections.

As in the preceding section, in each of those to follow the first part will be devoted to melodies whose fundamental note falls on the *second* degree; in the second part melodies whose fundamental note is on the *first* degree will be dealt with. This order is chosen in order to aid melodic hearing and to discourage any seeking after the major or other modal relations. It has already been remarked in the Introduction that modal relations will be discussed in the second part of the book.

1. *Given.* Four notes covering a fourth, with the fundamental note on the second degree.

Exercise. To compose a melody with the notes G-a-b-c, with *a* as fundamental note.

Analysis of Example 20. In the first two bars the tonal function is twice represented by the functional unit *c-a*, a function which offers no variety and a further repetition of which would be monotonous.

However, the third bar has the same statement again (*c-a*); but in the fourth bar, fortunately, appears an important variation, namely the introduction of a counter-note on the heavy beat of the bar. Thus in the first four bars we have (represented here only by the principal notes) the statement: *ca-ca / ca-b-a.*

Now it is also desirable that there should be variation in the movement of the intervals [7]. While the first four bars contained descending figures, the fifth bar by way of change begins with a rising figure in which the *a* is accented, while in the sixth bar the *a* is established as fundamental note by its lower second G. In the fifth bar *b* twice appears as a prosodic note of *a*. Bar 6 begins with G, which is heard as the lower prosodic note of *a*, and consequently in *this* rhythmical context the *b* (at the end of the fifth bar) and G (at the beginning of the sixth bar) are not heard so strongly in the function of contrasting third; as far as there is any functional contrast, this calls for the *a*.

In the seventh bar attention is directed to the third *b*-G which, after the preceding confirmation of *a* as fundamental note and introduced by the opposite pole of *a* in the functional unit *a*-*c*, namely *c*, leaves no other note than *a* to be expected. When, therefore, the final bar begins with the counter-note *b* of the fundamental note, this expectation is momentarily disappointed, only, however, to strengthen the necessity for the final appearance of *a*.

Analysis of Example 21. The first bar contains the statement *a*-*c*, the second the return to *a* but with the occurrence of *b* as prosodic note, contrasting with the interpolar tension of the third-group *a*-*c*. The third bar calls attention to the contrasting third G-*b* of the principal third, thus insisting on a transition to *a*. This *a* could have been repeated (*a*-*a*) but the rise to *b* indicates that we have here only a half-close.

The fifth and sixth bars contain as their most important contribution the statement *c*-*a* / *a*-*c*, yet clever use is made of the functions of the counter-notes, among other things producing the counter-third *b*-G and thereby avoiding all trace of monotony in the repetition of the principal third.

How greatly both the order of the notes and the rhythm influence the melodic functions appears from the succession *b*-G in the transition from the fifth to the sixth bar.

In Example 20 we saw in the same place (bars 5 and 6) that the *b* at the end of bar 5 was a prosodic note of the preceding *a*, and that the G at the beginning of bar 6 was a prosodic note of the following *a*-*a*. The notes *b* and G thus each had an independent function and were therefore scarcely felt to constitute together a contrasting third.

In Example 21 the function of *b*-G is different. In bar 5 here the first *b* in the succession *c*-*b*-*a* is a transitional note with linking function. The second *b* in the same bar can be regarded as a transitional note to G, in which case the *b*-G is already to some extent heard as a contrasting third in regard to the following *a*. This contrast would have been stronger if bars 5 and 6 had run: *acab* / *Gaa*- /, for then the *b*-G, with *a*-*c*-*a* preceding and *a* following in bar 6, would have been felt more clearly as a contrasting third. These are nuances which help to make the ear more sensitive to the melodic functions; such details may at first, perhaps, cause some uncertainty, but further acquaintance will show that an analysis of this sort is not difficult.

[7] Guido of Arezzo called attention to this necessity in about the year 1025, and ever since this idea has been enshrined in the maxim *Musica est motus vocum* ("Music is a movement of notes").

For there are only two melodic principles in question here, that of the prosodic note and of the contrasting third, although it must be noted that the order of the notes and their rhythmical placing also play a part in determining the functions and their relative strength, which both depend on the stronger or weaker accentuation of the notes concerned (see pp. 25 and 27).

In the seventh and eighth bars, on account of the form (four bars opening section, four bars closing section), the ear expects a cadence. At this point, therefore, something should be said about melodic cadence.

The cadence (from the Latin *cádere,* "to fall") is the melodic ending of a melody on the fundamental note as its point of repose.

A strong melodic cadence resembles a harmonic cadence in as far as in both the "fall" to the closing note or chord is prepared for by a preceding functional contrast, a functional tension demanding resolution on the final note or chord. We are already familiar with the functions which in a melody give rise to contrast or tension, namely (1) the counter-note or prosodic note, and (2) the contrasting third.

Accordingly in a strong melodic cadence the final note is preceded either by a counter-note or by a contrasting third. The scheme of a strong melodic cadence therefore involves the following succession of notes: (1) fundamental note or principal third, (2) counter-note or contrasting third, (3) fundamental note.

The term "strong" cadence is used here deliberately, as other, weak, melodic cadences are also possible; these are discussed in Note 1 below.

To return now to the cadence of Example 21, we see that bar 6 ends with the third, which in the preceding bars has been heard as the principal third of the melody, thus satisfying the form of cadence given as No. 1 above. Bars 7 and 8 form a contrasting-third cadence of the form (expressed in principal notes) *G-b-b-a;* that is, contrasting third + fundamental note, Nos. 2 + 3 of the cadence formation mentioned above.

The principal notes *G-b-b-a* are supplemented by *a* and *c,* which are merely required to strengthen the function of the contrasting third and so may not occur on a heavy or relatively heavy beat of the bar.

In bar 7 *a* is also a transitional note functionally linking *G* and *b,* and *c* is a prosodic note of *b.* The whole constitutes accordingly a cadence which in respect of clarity leaves nothing to be desired; that is to say, after *Gabc/b-* nothing else but the fundamental note can possibly follow to conclude the melody.

Observation. After what has been said earlier about the functional unit of the third (e.g., *a-c,* the two notes of which exhibit an interpolar tension) and about the contrasting notes of this third (the lower second G and the b between the two notes of the third), we meet here the principle of a contrasting third (G-b) of the principal third (a-c).

Law. If four notes are given covering a perfect fourth and with the fundamental note on the second degree, the second and fourth degrees constitute an interpolar functional unit on the fundamental note, in relation to which the other degrees, one and three, each function *separately* as counter-notes (prosodic notes) with an urge towards resolution on degrees 2 and 4 respectively, while *together* they form a counter-third with an urge towards resolution on the notes of the principal third (2 and 4). This last is called the contrasting third (1 and 3) of the principal third (2 and 4).

Law. A melody is an interplay between on the one hand the fundamental note and the notes which form a functional unit with it and on the other hand the contrasting notes of those just mentioned, an interplay in which (in an extended melody) the fundamental note must triumph and in which the functions of rhythm and form help in determining the laws to be followed.

Every *good*, that is to say, competent, *justified* melody (in the sense in which one speaks of a musically justified harmonisation) is a revelation of the infinite possibilities offered in this interplay by an observation of the laws. A *beautiful* melody astonishes by its originality, its unity, its mastery of old or choice of new laws; it is the perfect reflection in sound of a personal emotion, a marvellous and surprising discovery out of an unlimited number of possibilities and hence the work of genius.

Note 1. The theory of cadences is important. Every good melody should have a cadence which arises naturally out of its own structure. If the form of the cadence is considered in itself, a distinction can be made between stronger and weaker cadences. Taking the material considered so far, with the fundamental note on the first or second degree, the cadence-forms can be arranged in order of decreasing strength as follows (a being the fundamental note):

1. with the contrasting third of the fundamental note: *c-a-b-G-a* or *a-c-b-G-a*;
2. with a counter-note of the fundamental note: *a-G-a* or *a-b-a*;
3. with the functional unit of the principal third: *a-c-a*;
4. with a repetition of the fundamental note: *a-a*.

Mixtures of these cadence-types can also occur. Experiment with these, also with G (in *G-a-b-c*) as fundamental note.

The function of rhythm is also important in the formation of cadences.

In many cases the note leading up to the fundamental note must

36

fall on a heavy or relatively heavy beat of the bar, or even fill a whole bar; in free rhythm it must give rise to at least some slight rhythmical tension. If in Example 21 the second half of the melody were to be cbab/Gac-/Gacb/a-, one would expect as final note G rather than a, as a comes on the heavy beat of the bar. If on the other hand the melody were cbab/Gac-/Gacb/G-, then a conclusion on a rather than on G would be expected, as in the last bar G comes on the heavy beat.

Note 2. Below is the tune sung to cure the sick by the Indians of the Taulipang tribe in Central Guiana (Brazil).

E. M. v Hornbostel

At first sight one would seem to have little to go on in analysing this remarkable melody, with its uncertain placing of the G. This varying G must be regarded as a floating note between F and a. F is the fundamental note but at first (as in many European children's songs) it is not heard. After some interplay between a and G the identity of the fundamental note is made clear by the introduction of Eb as its lower second. The floating note G functions first as the lower prosodic note of a and later as the upper prosodic note of F. This example illustrates how the functional laws are applied and shows also how on close inspection analysis is not at all a difficult matter.

2. *Given.* Four notes covering a fourth, with the fundamental note on the first degree.

Exercise. To compose a melody with the notes G-a-b-c, with G as fundamental note.

Analysis. The first four bars establish the fundamental note and bring into relief the functional tension between the fundamental note and the third above it (*G-b*). In the fifth bar is heard the contrasting third (*c-a*), in the sixth the principal third; in these two bars there is thus a contrast between two thirds. Just as a prosodic note leads one to expect a return to the dominating note and a contrasting third calls for resolution on one of the notes of the principal third, so after a contrast between two thirds the ear desires a resolution on one of the notes of the first third; that is to say, after *c-a / b-G* a resolution on *a* [8]. This *a* is a suitable note for a melodic half-close and therefore we get the figure *a-b-a*, in which *b* functions as a prosodic note of *a*.

The *a* of bar 8 contains an indication to the ear that the melody, whose fundamental note is *G*, is not yet finished. We may note in passing that a melody in the first half (bars 1-4) of the opening section of which it is mainly the principal third that is heard, demands a half-close (bar 8) on one of the counter-notes. Attention is called to this because, *considered by itself*, after the principal third (*G-b*) in bars 1-4 descent (*b-G*) migt very well follow in bars 4-8, thus — *b a / G b / a-/ G-//*. But the melody would then be finished, which was not the intention. This example will suffice to explain the following law: The more the opening section of a melody stresses the notes of the principal third, the more desirable it becomes that the half-close should fall on a counter-note.

To return to the example given above, in bars 9 and 10 (note the heavy beats) the principal third (*b-G*) is stressed. In bar 9 *a* is a transitional note to *G* (functional linking of *b-a-G*). In bar 10 there are various possibilities of transition from *a*. Here it is chosen as a foundation for the counter-third *a-c-a* (bars 10-11). Thus bars 9-11 contain a contrasting interplay of thirds: *b-G-a-c-a*; such an interplay always requires a resolution (see above) on one of the notes of the first third, in this case *b*.

The last four bars contain an example of a strong composite cadence — first a contrasting-third cadence (*c-a-b-G*), followed by a counter-note cadence (*a-G*). In this way all uncertainty is removed about the choice of the final note.

Observation. There is nothing new here in the way of functional relations. The thirds are functional units together contrasting mutually, and one of them also contrasts with one of the notes of the other. As regards terminology we have principal third (*G-b*) and contrasting third (*a-c*), and the functional opposition produced by the immediate succession of these thirds is called the contrast of thirds.

---

[8] The reverse is also true: after *b-G-a-c* the ear desires a return either, preferably, to *b*, or to *G*.

Law. Given four notes covering a perfect fourth and with the fundamental note on the first degree, then degrees 1 and 3 constitute an interpolar functional unit in relation to which degrees 2 and 4 function *separately* as counter-notes and *together* as a contrasting third (*c-a*) over against the principal third (*b-G*).

Exercises. As a new exercise, compose a melody with the notes *a-b-c-d* and *a* as fundamental note, and with *F-G-a-b* and *G* as fundamental note (but avoid the tritone!).

Although theoretically possible, it is in practice difficult in performance to work out the exercises in this section with the fundamental note on the third and fourth degrees.

Exercises with other series of three and four notes than those given in the exercises above are, of course, also possible but, as has been recommended in the Introduction, it is better not to attempt them until after the chapter on the principles of euphony.

Note. To conclude this section here is an analysis of one of the simplest and most beautiful of love-songs, an old version of "Schoon lief, hoe ligt gij hier" ("Fair love, how liest thou here"). The notes are *CDEF* (equivalent to *Gabc*), with *D* as fundamental note.

Analysis. In the first three bars we have the functional unit of the principal third *D-F-D*, with variation provided by *E* as a transitional note and with the fundamental note confirmed by the presence of the prosodic note *C*. The next section also begins with this functional unit but by way of variation starts on the upper third *F*. On the word *dreaming* (*droome*) there must be a half-close. If either *D* or *F* were chosen for this, not only would there be too little variety but also the effect of a half-close would not be satisfactorily achieved. To attain this one of the notes of the counter-third (*E* or *C*) must be selected. Now as the first section contains a rise and a fall (*D-F-D*) and the second section begins with a fall (*F-D*), a rise to *E* for the final note of this second section is more satisfactory than a descent to C. The closing section begins with the counter-note of *D*, namely *E*, a welcome change after the strong stressing of *D-F* in the opening section. Moreover it is made clear in this way that this is the beginning of the second part of the melody. The counter-note is now varied by the principal third (*D F D*), and after this succession of counter-note and principal third one of the counter-notes (*E* or *C*) is expected. And if for structural reasons the end of the first section (on *dreaming, droome*) required a rise to *E*, now, on account of its structural parallelism with the first half of the opening section, the conclusion (on *to May, ontfaan*) requires a descent to C.

The closing section runs parallel to that which precedes (*Rise up and bid good day, wilt opstaan en de Mei*), that is to say, it begins on the counter-note C and then has the same rise and fall (*D E F D*). In order to make a perfect preparation for the cadence C-D, the sequence *F-D-C-D-* is subdivided into *F-ED-C-D* (thus making use of the notes of the contrasting third *E-C*). *E-C-D* would make a strong cadence, but in *this* context *F-ED-C-D* is much more effective.

One can see from this analysis how finely conceived this melody is and also how much more natural it is in this version than in the better-known form with notes of smaller value and with the C twice replaced by the modern lower fourth *A*.

§ 4. The functional affinities of five given notes

1. *Given.* Five notes covering a perfect fifth, with the fundamental note on the second degree.

Exercise. To compose a melody with the notes *G-a-b-c-d*, with *a* as fundamental note.

Analysis. The first two bars contain the statement *a-c-a* with *b* in linking function and *G* as prosodic note of *a*, the unit of the principal third (*a-c-a*) being sufficiently varied by the use of *b* and *G*, which also establishes *a* as the fundamental note. What is wanted now is a further variation of the principal third. This is provided by the contrasting thirds (or contrasting fifth), namely *G-b-d*, of the principal third *a-c* (read bar 3 as *b-G-b-d*). The half-close of the melody comes on *b*, but not until *c* has been heard stressed as a counter-note preparing for *b*.

After the first two bars have fixed attention on the fundamental note *a* and the next two bars on its counter-note *b*, in bars 5 and 6 prominence is given to the upper second of *b*, namely *c*. From this *c* there is a descent to *a*, the two forming a functional unit which is varied on the lighter beats of the bar by the contrasting notes *d* and *b* in their function of prosodic notes (*cdcbc*), the result being that *after* the principal third *c-a* has been heard, one of the contrasting notes is expected.

In bar 6, therefore, there is a descent to the lower second of the fundamental note, by way of preparation for the concluding section.

In the last two bars a cadence is formed on the contrasting notes *b* and *G*, which coming after what has preceded call for *a* as the final note.

A melody constructed out of these notes should also, of course, be able to make use of the interval of the fifth, *G-d-G*. The function of this fifth-interval should be investigated in some succession of notes by way of experiment (for more about this see pp. 49-50).

It need hardly be said that such leaps of a fifth are hardly suitable in vocal melodies in this simple folksong style.

Observation. The fundamental note *a* has a contrasting third in *b-G*, and the principal third *a-c* contrasts with both *b-G* and *b-d*. As the two notes *a-c* constitute a functional unit which in the melodic interplay needs to be varied by the use of counter-notes, these in turn form functional units of thirds (*G-b* and *b-d*) and also of a fifth (*G-d*) contrasting with the principal third *a-c*.

Law. Given five notes covering a perfect fifth and with the fundamental note on the second degree, then degrees 2 and 4 constitute an interpolar functional unit on the fundamental note, in relation to which degrees 1, 3 and 5, taken separately, function as counter-notes requiring resolution on the notes of the principal third; while degrees 1 and 3, and 3 and 5, function together in pairs as contrasting thirds requiring the same resolution; and degrees 1 and 5 together have the function of a contrasting fifth also demanding resolution on the notes of the principal third — which in this case, therefore, has two contrasting thirds and one contrasting fifth.

Note. This section, like the preceding, will also be concluded with an analysis of a classical melody, this time a Gregorian chant, the Introit of the first Mass on Christmas Day.

This richly ornamented art-melody (the modern notation gives only an approximate indication of the original performance of certain vocal ornaments now no longer in use) can be reduced to its principal notes by omitting the transitional notes and the functionally unimportant decorative figures such as repeated notes. This reduction to its principal notes is essential with most melodies if one is to get a clear idea of the melodic tonal functions. Reduced to its principal notes, the above example appears as follows:

Analysis. The opening on *Dominus* gives clearly the functional unit of the principal third (*D-F-D*), accented by the prosodic note *G*, thus producing the figure *D-F-G-F* (the so-called modal repercussion of the plagal Dorian, or Hypodorian, mode). The principal third is repeated on *dixit* but on *ad* we have the counter-third (*C-E*) of the fundamental note *D*, leading to resolution on the latter, which is thereby sufficiently established as the fundamental note. On *filius* we have a figure based on *D* which reduces to *DECD*. On *meus* attention is directed to the upper third of the fundamental note, namely *F*. As the composer wishes to construct his melody in two main sections or sentences of which the first ends on *es tu*, there must be a half-close on these words.

Up till now we have had almost exclusively the principal third, so now follows a half-close on one of the counter-notes of the fundamental note and this the most important, namely the lower second *C*. This is prepared for by the figure *DEDC* on the word *es*. (Here and in the pages that follow, by half-close must always be understood the *melodic* half-close).

The second sentence begins with the same figure as the first, namely the principal third (on *ego ho-*); as this is the last section before the close it also ends on the counter-note, namely the lower second (*DC-C*). The following figure *DEC* is a confirmation of *D* that resolves either on *D* or on its third *F*. The *F* is chosen in order to lead to the cadence. There follows a strong (and original) cadence that makes use of the counter-third and the principal third: *GE-FD*. In several manuscripts this *F* is given as a lengthened note in contrast with the group *GFE*, thus once more stressing the functional unit of the principal third.

This example is particularly instructive as showing how in the Gregorian modes it is possible to speak of a *dominans* which can be a minor third above the tonic. The interpolar tension between the fundamental note and the third above is similar to the relationship between the keynote and the fifth above in melodies in the major and minor keys. But is there no interpolar tension between the thirds in these last? Of course there is, but it is very much weaker, owing to the adoption of the triad as a unit. Owing to the domination of the fifth in the triad the tension between the tonic and the third above it (the mediant), and in general between the first and third degrees of a triad, is considerably weakened. Thus in the present example, play the triad *D-F-a* with the first note *D* and observe how the interesting interplay with the following third *F* loses greatly in effect. In its horizontal, melodic form the principle of the triad was not unknown to the composers of plainsong (as was of course the vertical triad as a polyphonic unit), but known to them equally, if not in stronger measure, was the principle of the *two-note* unit, in the form of the interpolar tension of the third, and it is to this conception of the third that in its method the theory of melody must return.

Note 2. From the point of view of method it is better to postpone the writing of melodies of five notes and more with the *do* and *fa* degrees as fundamental notes, since it is difficult for the ear trained in harmony to free itself from the principle of the triad, with its tonic and dominant and the functional relations obtaining between them.

The method followed in this book is based first and foremost on purely melodic listening and this is continued as long as possible. The writing of melodies covering a fifth and with the fundamental note on the *do* or *fa* degree is accordingly only to be recommended if it can be carried out purely from the point of view of melody.

2. *Given.* Five notes covering a perfect fifth and with the fundamental note on the first degree.

Exercise (taking into account the remark just made above). To compose a melody with the notes *G-a-b-c-d*, with *G* as fundamental note.

Analysis. The first section consists of an ornamentation of the principal notes G-b-G. To be noticed is the *a* in the function of counternote of the principal third at the beginning of bar 2. The second section is an ornamentation of the descending fifth G-d-b-G [9], once again with the counter-note *a* (accented by the figure a-G-a) before the closing note G of bar 4. The third section has as its principal notes G-(c)-a-c-a-b-d. One feels how after the stressing of the notes of the principal thirds (G-b-d-d-G) in the first two sections, the accenting of the contrasting third *a-c* in this third section comes as a happy variation.

The fourth section contains the final cadence, which is a repetition of the second section with one slight change. The principal notes of this last section are *d-b-d-a-G* or, further shortened, *d-b-a-G*. The whole section gives clear prominence to the unit of the principal third and of the fifth on the fundamental note (henceforth to be termed the principal fifth), to which the notes of the third on the second degree (*a-c*) both separately and together form a contrast.

[9] At the risk of stressing the harmonic element — which is the last thing to be desired here (see § 7 on page 19) — it may be pointed out in passing that *melodically* the accented *d* of bar 3 forms a unit with the fundamental note, while *harmonically* it functions as a dominant. On this difference and the reason for it see Chapter III, §§ 3 and 5.

If anyone should be interested in seeing how this melody was set polyphonically in the Middle Ages, below is a two-part setting of the fourteenth century which must have been familiar over a wide area in Holland and Germany. It is still to be found several times in the unisonal song-books of the seventeenth century, either with the second part or in a mixture of the two parts. In the form that follows the principal melody is given, transposed and altered, in the lower part.

Although the polyphony of this piece will become clearer after the section "From

Law. Given five notes covering a perfect fifth and with the fundamental note on the first degree, then degrees 1 and 3, 3 and 5, and 1 and 5 form interpolar functional units on the fundamental note, to which degrees 2 and 4, either separately or as a third, constitute a contrast. If this functional contrast, which is so requisite for the sake of melodic variety, occurs, then a return is required to the notes of the principal thirds or the principal fifth.

Note. No reference has so far been made to the application of this method in musical instruction in schools. It is clear, however, that if functional hearing is to be taught, there are all sorts of ways of achieving this end. One can play song-games by writing up on the board two groups of notes (the principal third or thirds and the contrasting third or thirds) and getting songs sung by pointing successively to the different degrees. Or one can let different groups in the class each represent a single note and have them sing a melody by pointing from one group to another; the same thing can be played as a ball-game in which the child receiving the ball sings a note previously decided upon. Or one can give the beginning of a melody and have it completed impromptu in various ways — and so on. There are many ways of illustrating the functional laws visually; e.g. the idea of a prosodic note can be represented by a train which instead of taking the direct route makes a détour; or colours that match to represent the notes of the principal third can be placed side by side with contrasting colours representing the counter-notes; and all sorts of different diagrams can be used.

melody to harmony" (page 76 following) has been reached, there follow here, in connection with what has just been said, a few notes explaining the rather strange "harmonisation".

1. The first and the last note of each of the four sections is regarded as a melodic note, not as harmony. In the early centuries of European polyphony the polyphonic principle developed out of melody: phenomena such as opening and closing *chords* therefore appear only much later. Accordingly, one began and finished just with the note of the melody or with this and its octave.

2. The polyphonic cadences of this period must also be considered melodically and not harmonically. The starting-point is the principle of the melodic counter-third cadence and, as the melody must end on the fundamental note (or the fundamental note and its octave), in the earliest two-part writing the fundamental note was preceded by its counter-third. If the fundamental note is C, then the preceding "chord" consists of B and D (at the close in octaves D and the high b leading to c). Originally this was certainly not heard as latent dominant-tonic cadence. More will be said about the latter in § 3 of Chapter III.

3. In polyphonic music in popular style, like this piece, fifths are generally preferred, but sometimes, for the sake of variety or on account of the melodic progression, other intervals also occur.

4. We may be sure that the polyphony of this piece is well considered and at the time of its composition passed for competent, although we regard it now as primitive polyphony or heterophony.

§ 5. The functional affinities of six given notes

1. *Given.* Six notes covering a major or minor sixth and with the fundamental note on the second degree.

Exercise. To compose a melody with the notes G-a-b-c-d-e and with *a* as fundamental note.

Analysis. The first bar contains as its principal statement a-b-d-c-a-b, the last note of which, *b*, indicates a continuation of the melody. The fundamental note *a* or, *c* being accented, the principal third c-a is preceded by its contrasting third b-d. In the second bar we have c-d-b. It is curious that the last five notes of the first and second bars are the same although their functions are different. Compare, e.g., the functions of *b* and *a*, the third and second notes respectively before the last. The first time this *a* has the function of a principal note in the descending sequence c-(b)-a, while the immediately preceding *b* is a transitional note; the second time *b* is a principal note and the following *a* serves to confirm or accent it, thus acting as a prosodic note of *b*.

In the third bar c-e-c-b-G are the principal notes, and the two principal thirds c-e-c-(a) are followed by the contrasting third b-G. The fourth bar is a repetition of the first, but without the turn at the end to the counter-note *b*.

Observation. If six notes, G-a-b-c-d-e, are given, with *a* as fundamental note, then the thirds constitute units of such a kind that the principal thirds a-c and c-e, or both together (a-c-e), find in G-b-d their contrasting notes, contrasting thirds and contrasting fifth.

Law. Given six notes covering a major or minor sixth and with the fundamental note on the second degree, then degrees 2, 4 and 6 constitute a unit of interpolar tension on the fundamental note (principal thirds and principal fifth), in contrast with which degrees 1, 3 and 5 have separately the function of counter-notes while in combination they form contrasting thirds and a contrasting fifth. We thus have in addition to the principle of counter-notes and contrasting thirds a new functional relationship in the contrast of the perfect fifth, i.e. the opposition of principal fifth and contrasting fifth.

2. *Given.* Six notes covering a major or minor sixth and with the fundamental note on the first degree.

Exercise. To compose a melody with the notes G-*a-b-c-d-e,* with G as fundamental note.

Analysis. The form of this melody, which consists of four sections, is a, a, b, b'. In section "a" we have the two principal thirds, ending on the principal fifth (G-*b-d,* with *e* as prosodic note of *d*). The third section ("b") provides the requisite variation by adding the contrasting thirds *c-e* and *a-c,* which interchange with the principal third *b-d.* The fourth section ("b' "), which has to descend to the fundamental note, alters the group *a-b-c* of bar 11 to *a-b-a* (bar 15), with *b* as prosodic note accenting *a,* which is the counter-note of the fundamental note G.

Observation. We can now add to what has already been stated, that with six notes whose first degree is the fundamental note use can also be made of two principal thirds or a principal fifth contrasting functionally with two contrasting thirds or a contrasting fifth.

Law. Given six notes covering a major or minor sixth and with the fundamental note on the first degree, then degrees 1, 3 and 5 form units of interpolar tension (principal thirds and principal fifth), in contrast with which degrees 2, 4 and 6 have separately the function of counter-notes, while their combinations constitute contrasting thirds and a contrasting fifth [10].

Note 1. If a melody such as the well-known childrens' song

is examined from the point of view of the laws of functional affinity established so far, an analysis would run as follows. In the first two

---

[10] An example in which the contrasting fifths are more prominent will be found on page 49.

bars there is a rise from the fundamental note to the principal fifth. The third bar stresses strongly the prosodic note *e* of the fifth (*d*). In the movement of these four bars the first notes of the first and third bars are strongly accented; from a functional point of view this is due to the fact that the first and third bars represent tension or effort while the second and fourth bars represent relief or achievement. Account is also taken of this in the descent from *c* to *G* in the last four bars.

The motor tension of the uneven bars 1 and 3 is continued in bars 5 and 7. Now after attention has been directed to the principal fifth *G-d*, in bars 5 and 7 preference will naturally be given to the notes of the counter-third *c-a*. This is what happens, and although this little tune is not very original, yet in accordance with the functional relationships it contains a melodic interplay that satisfies the laws and a musically justified melody is the result.

This example raises the question whether this melodic theory would give any help in harmonising a melody. A full answer to this question would anticipate what will be said later about melodies in the major key. Yet it is interesting to note that the melodic functions which have here been revealed do provide indications for a simple harmonisation.

The first two bars contain the triad *G-b-d*. The third bar stresses *d* by means of the prosodic note *e*; the same effect would have been produced by using the prosodic note *c*, although then one would have expected *b* to follow, a note which nevertheless, like *d*, is one of the principal thirds. The note *e* is thus functionally identical with *c*, so that in the third bar one could at least have the two-note "chord" *c-e*.

The fourth bar returns to *d* and to the function *G-b-d*. The fifth bar begins by accenting the counter-third *c-a*. The note *b* in bar 6 is one of the principal thirds (*G-b-d*). Bar 7 stresses the counter-note of the fundamental note, which has another counter-note in the lower second. Granted that the melody is in major and has *f♯* as lower second, then according to the melodic laws considered so far we must have the two-note "chord" *f♯-a* supplemented by the upper fifth, *c*, which belongs to it. This is as far as we can go at present, for from what we have had so far we cannot yet use the tetrachord with which our ears are so familiar, the chord of the seventh on the fifth degree which resolves in the triad on the fundamental note. Although this last has still to be discussed, in the meantime we may be satisfied with the knowledge of the triad *f♯-a-c* which we have discovered to be the contrasting triad of the triad on the fundamental note.

Later it will be proved historically that the cadence consisting of contrasting triad plus principal triad was the usual form of cadence in melodies in the old ecclesiastical modes, in contrast with the V-I triad-order which is so familiar to us.

To sum up, the question whether the theory of melody can be a useful foundation for harmony can be answered in the affirmative, for the following reasons. First, one ought to learn how to compose a melody before learning to harmonise one. Second, a method such as this sharpens one's awareness of the functional relations which the notes of a melody bear to one another mutually. Third, there is a relationship (and not merely an historical one) between these melodic functional affinities and the principles of harmony. Fourth, in order to learn to harmonise or to accompany melodies in the old ecclesiastical modes it is, if not absolutely essential, at least of the very greatest use to have some understanding of the functional affinities in melody. Here, indeed, we are anticipating matters which have still to be discussed, but this example offered a welcome opportunity of stressing now the connection between melody and harmony.

Note 2. If it has been said that it is better at first not to practise writing melodies of four and five notes with the fundamental note on the fourth or fifth degree, this *can* be done on these degrees with melodies of six, seven, and more notes. For example, in compositions in the plagal modes it is very common for the fundamental note (the tonic) to be the fourth degree when the melody has a range of a sixth or an octave. Yet it is better, for the reasons given earlier, for the time being not to choose a fundamental note which has a minor second below it.

Note 3. It has already been pointed out that in general wide intervals should be avoided in simple melodies of folksong type. It also goes without saying that it is difficult to construct melodies in which the principle of the contrast of fifths is dominant. For this, one has to have exercises like the following:

Here is an example of a melody with contrast of fifths:

Example. (Given six notes, G-a-b-c-d-e, with G as fundamental note):

Analysis. In the first bar we have a balancing of functionally identical notes (*G d b G*) with a linking *a* between. The second bar maintains this principal function. As no contrasting function occurs at any rhythmically important point in them, the third bar and the first half of the fourth bar are still felt as functions of the fundamental note (i.e. as functional units of this); but the ear sensitive to form is so expectant of a change of function at the half-close that the second *b* in bar 4 is already heard as a prosodic note accenting the counter-note *a*!

The fifth bar takes over the contrasting function in a balancing functional unit *e a c e*. After this long-awaited and then maintained contrasting function, the function of the principal note in bar 6 is normal (the *d-b* being felt as a functional unit) and this is also maintained, as at the beginning, to the end of the seventh bar. The conclusion is now expected, being preceded, by way of confirmation, by a contrasting function, *c-a*. (A less conventional progression in bars 3 and 7 would be *d-cbed*).

Observation. *G d b G* are heard as a functional unit, as are also *e a c e*, which together have contrasting function. Although (on page 46) the principle of the contrast of fifths has already been formulated as a law, here is the same law as derived directly from the above example and therefore in a different form: In a melody of six notes a fifth is felt to constitute itself, over and above its constituent thirds, a functional unit with its root; the fifth on the fundamental note is the principal fifth, the other is the contrasting fifth.

Note 4. (arising out of Ex. 33). It is interesting in this example to compare the harmonies which are heard melodically when the melody is sung by itself, with those which have to be introduced when the melody is harmonised.

If the melody is heard by itself, then for the first three and a half bars one is conscious only of the functions of the principal note; the *b-a* of the half-close is heard as a contrasting function accented by the prosodic note. The *e* of bar 5 (and with it the whole bar) acts as a contrasting function which links up perfectly with the *a* of the half-close. The sixth bar (*d-c-b--*) is entirely a fundamental-note function. This can be tested by substituting *d-b g--*; for *d-c b--*: the function of both *d*'s is the same — clearly a principal-note function.

If now one sets about harmonising the melody in such a way that the melodic functions are maintained as far as possible, then several difficulties arise.

1. The prosodic note *e* in the third bar. (a) This can be regarded as the third of the subdominant triad *c e g* with *c* as root. But then the prosodic note *e* becomes unpleasantly heavier than is melodically intended. (b) It can also be regarded as a passing-note not affecting the harmony, but in this case it loses practically all its original significance as a prosodic note accenting the principal fifth *d*.

2. The *a* of the half-close and the *e-a c d e* of the fifth bar. (a) In a harmonisation it is natural to regard the *b-a* of bar 4 as part of a dominant triad with a suspension; but *e-a c* in bar 5 are the constituent notes of the triad on the second degree (*a*) — so that the *a*'s in these two bars have *different* functions, which is certainly not the case in the original melody. (b) This difficulty can be avoided by regarding both *a*'s as members of a chord of the dominant ninth (root *d*) with no change of function, and by putting under the first *a*

50

a *d* and under the second an *f♯* in the bass. But there are other objections against this. First, the progression *b-a // e-a*, etc., becomes harmonically much heavier than it is melodically; and secondly, the incomplete chord of the dominant ninth under the *e* of the fifth bar (with *f♯* as bass) can be resolved in a subdominant triad under the *cde* of the melody (bass note *e* 6) and a dominant triad under the *d-c* of bar 6 (bass note *f♯* 6). But the melody has none of these radical changes of function: bar 5 is one functional unit (contrasting function), bar 6 another (principal function). (c) If these melodic functional units are to be preserved in the harmony (*e-a* above *f♯* 7, *cde* above *a* 6, *d-c* above *b* 6, *b--* above *g* 3), then the balancing of these units (*ea-ce* and *db*) loses much of its effect.

Anyhow, all the notes of the melody are already heard vertically in the chord used in the harmonising of the groups.

This can be made clear by a single example. Let us take bar 5. Melodically we hear successively the descent from the prosodic note *e* to its lower fifth *a* (functional unit of the fifth), then a rise to *c* and from *c* (*via d* as transitional note) to the upper fifth *e*. We thus have a melodic statement made by means of a sequence of different units (*e-a / a-c / c-e*).

Now what does the harmony do? It collects these notes together (with the first note *e* is heard a chord such as *f♯-a-c-e* with the latent root *d*), thus betraying immediately everything that the melody contains in the way of surprise.

It is clear from this how important it is to listen carefully to a melody before harmonising it. But above all it confirms the claim made in the Preface that the melodic functions cannot always be brought completely into line with the harmonic functions. Only if a melody is listened to according to its own melodic laws — and this is its right — can the difficulties of harmonisation pointed out above be explained.

This gives occasion to point out also the very great difference there is between a melody constructed melodically and one derived from harmony. The latter as it is worked out theoretically (cp. many harmony exercises by professional students) consists of the top notes of a series of chords: such "melodies" have little connection with living monophonic melody.

Note 5. The following example represents a very well known melodic scheme that occurs both in plainsong and in many Dutch and Flemish folksongs.

Analyse this melody. We have here a mixture of the so-called Mixolydian-plagal (Hypomixolydian) and the Phrygian-plagal (Hypophrygian) modes, but with a preference for the Phrygian which is prominent at the end of the second and fourth sections.

If the third section had ended with *ab / G* instead of *ba / G*, i.e. with the heavy beat on the counter-note (*a*) of G, the latter would have had more markedly the character of a final cadence. The same change, but at the end of the fourth section, would allow for a close on G but it would not be very satisfying owing to the fact that G already occurs at the end of the third section and is there felt as a half-close. It is also possible to end the melody on G and yet still preserve a regular structure, by continuing after the first two sections (but preferably beginning with G/G instead of b/G) as follows:

The end $(bc / ba / G)$ of this altered version has purposely been made the same as that of the third section in the original version. Yet there the G was not felt as the fundamental note because the *form* of the melody required a continuation. One can see from this how the form of the melody plays a part in determining the melodic functions.

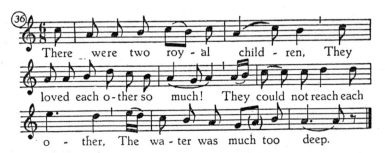

There _ were two roy - al child - ren, They loved each o - ther so much! They could not reach each o - ther, The wa - ter was much too deep.

Note 6. Here the opening section (up to *so much*) is mainly restricted to the notes of the principal third $(a\text{-}c\text{-}a)$, the third section to those of the third above $(c\text{-}e(c))$. One might regard the fundamental note of the opening section (a) as being transferred in the third section to the third above (c); after the functional unit $a\text{-}c\text{-}a$ varied by the counter-note b has been used in the opening section, the same thing is done in the third section with the third $c\text{-}e\text{-}c$. Such a method applies to melody the principle of transposition, and just as in harmony one could have I-V (V becoming I)-V-I (I becoming V)-I, so the displacement of the melodic centre here could be represented as follows: $I(a)\text{-}III(c)$ (III becoming I)$\text{-}III(e)\text{-}I(c)$ (I becoming III)$\text{-}I(a)$.

This sort of melodic transposition, here termed *transition*, occurs not infrequently in folksong melodies (and also in Gregorian chant). The less familiar version of *There were two royal children* given above is therefore to be analysed thus: at the beginning a is the fundamental note; then at the beginning of the concluding section there is transition, c becoming the new central note; and finally there is a return to the fundamental note.

From a melodic point of view a transition can be made to any note, but naturally there is a preference for a transition to the notes

52

most closely related in function to the fundamental note (principal function), namely its upper or lower third and its upper or lower fifth (see page 56). A special case of transition, namely in melodies in the major and minor keys, will be found on page 92 following, in connection with Example 52.

§ 6. The functional affinities of seven given notes

Note. In the case of seven given notes covering a major or minor seventh the application of a general law might give rise to misunderstanding or fear. Will account be taken here of the principles of the octave-unit and the function of the leading note?

We have not yet reached the end of this course. Although essentially the law that follows applies to both a major and a minor seventh (in the first case with certain restrictions to be dealt with later), in this section, in order to avoid misunderstanding, only the minor seventh will be discussed, it being understood as usual that we are concerned only with the diatonic scale, without accidentals.

Given. Seven notes covering a minor seventh, with the fundamental note on the second degree.

Exercise. To compose a melody with the notes G-a-b-c-d-e-f and with *a* as fundamental note.

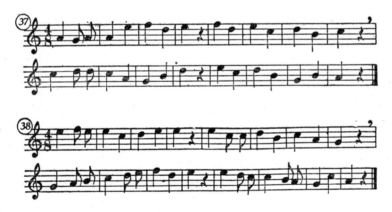

Observation. These examples suffice to show that degrees 2, 4 and 6 on the fundamental note contrast with the counter-notes 1, 3, 5 and 7 in such a way that a chain of three thirds can contrast with a chain, in this case, of two principal thirds. It goes without saying that if G is selected as fundamental note then degrees 1, 3, 5 and 7 contrast with degrees 2, 4 and 6.

Law. Given seven notes covering a minor seventh and with the

53

fundamental note on the second degree, then the thirds and the fifth of degrees 2, 4 and 6 act as functional units in relation to which the separate notes, the thirds and the fifths of degrees 1, 3, 5 and 7 have contrasting function. If the fundamental note is on the first degree, then there is the same contrast between degrees 1, 3, 5 and 7 on the one hand and degrees 2, 4 and 6 on the other.

§ 7. The functional affinities of eight and more given notes

After what we have had so far it will not be difficult to work out exercises of the same sort with eight and more notes (with a minor seventh, i.e. with a major second between the seventh and eighth degrees) and to see that the same general laws apply. According as the fundamental note is on the first, second, third or fourth degree, the interplay of the melody will be between two groups of notes, on the one hand those of the series of thirds on the fundamental note (with fundamental note on the first degree 1, 3, 5, 7, 9; on the second degree — which is preferable in the exercises — 2, 4, 6, 8, 10), and on the other hand the counter-notes of the series of principal thirds (2, 4, 6, 8, 10 against 1, 3, 5, 7, 9 and *vice versa*). In addition to the contrast of thirds and fifth we can also have the principle of accentuation by means of prosodic notes of both of the principal thirds and the contrasting thirds, while further we have at our disposal transitional notes and ornaments such as repeated notes, apart from the variations resulting from transitions and certain rhythmical and formal dispositions.

Here, to sum up, is a fuller definition of melody than that given above on page 11: A melody consists of an interplay between on the one hand the fundamental note and the notes which form a functional unit with it (i.e. the series of thirds rising from the lower fifth [11] of the fundamental note) or are ornaments of it, and on the other hand the contrasting notes of the fundamental note and the notes which form functional units with these (i.e. the series of thirds rising from the lower fourth of the fundamental note). Besides the laws of the functions of tension and contrast, melody also has its laws of euphony, rhythm and form.

All these laws have been sufficiently illustrated except those of euphony, and these will be dealt with in the next chapter.

---

[11] In principle one can also say here "from the lower seventh of the fundamental note", and with reference to the contrasting thirds "from the lower sixth of the fundamental note". It still remains to be investigated whether (as I think likely) in melodies beyond a certain range, e.g. continuing the chain of thirds above the upper octave of the fundamental note, transition still occurs or ought to occur. Acoustics will be able to help solve this problem.

Exercises. 1. Analyse the Troubadour songs given in Examples 38a-c [12].

2. Analyse (but ignoring the fourths) Example 39, which is a part of a plainsong melody, noting how the principal-third series *D-F-a-c-e* is used in the *melisma*. Is such a melodic progression possible in the major or minor scale?

[12] The melody of the Donkey's Song of Sens, which in the Middle Ages was also provided with religious words, is used by Arthur Honegger as a *cantus firmus* in his *Joan of Arc at the Stake* (in the Trial scene, when the donkey is chosen as Clerk of the Court).

The analysis of this melody is made easier by referring to its principal notes, which are given in Example 40. Note that transition occurs on the high *c* immediately before the third phrase-mark. This *c* is established as a temporary tonal centre by the cadence *c-b-d-c*. A little later the tonal centre shifts *via a* to *F*.

The melodies selected so far have been built up on the principal-third series (on *D* e.g., *D-F-a-c-e*) and on the contrasting-third series of the lower second (on *D* e.g., *C-E-G-b-d-f*). Moreover we have learnt that the third *below* the fundamental note forms with this the same functional unit as the fundamental note with the third above. Hence continuing on these lines one can compose melodies which descend to the fifth below the fundamental note, in which case the two thirds formed by the lower fifth with the lower third and the lower third with the fundamental note constitute functional units with the same function as that of the principal thirds above the funda-mental note.

This is made clear in the following example, a *melisma* from the Sanctus of the "Ut-Re-Mi-Fa-So-La" Mass of Palestrina. It is to be noted that in the melodies he composed or revised (apart, i.e., from the themes he took over unchanged) Palestrina applies the laws of melodic function very consistently. Even if this is true in general of composers down to the sixteenth century, among them all Palestrina stands out as a model composer of classic melody. This is generally admitted, but only now is it clear why he is so, namely because he obeyed the natural laws of melody — even if, like the composers of plainsong, he did so unconsciously.

Analyse the following *melisma* by Palestrina (the tonic of the piece is *c*).

Conclusion. A word may be said in conclusion on the great advantages in both the teaching and practice of music of a knowledge of the functional laws of melody.

It is not only that the ear is trained in the conscious observation of the melodic functions and in the noting of the various gradations of strength in functions such as the functional unit and the contrasting function; the understanding of the form of a melody and the melodic structure of cadences is also helped by it. Such a training will be of the greatest use also in the performance of music, for it is just where the rhythm fails to give sufficient indications for good phrasing and for musical articulation or accent that an understanding of the melodic functions will point the way to the right interpretation. So, e.g., in melismata and cadences there must be an accentuation of the counter-notes, a detail which is often overlooked in the performance of melodic cadences, to which insufficient justice is thereby done. In this connection it is worth remarking that singers and performers on string and wind instruments generally have a much better feeling for melody and interpret it better than pianists and organists. The reason is that the former are occupied regularly with monophonic music, with melody.

The pianist can introduce phrasing into this harmonised music by making use of dynamically stronger or weaker successions of chords. This phrasing is in general justified, though it often has the disadvantage of diverting attention from the melody to the harmony, with the result that the rendering of the melody leaves much to be desired. The organist is faced by even greater difficulties in this respect, in as far as on his instrument the notes are all combined together in a single stream of sound and a dynamic accentuation of particular notes is impossible; he has to make himself master of a very special technique in order to do justice to the musical accentuation, that is, the musical rendering of the melody. It can therefore be a great help to students of the keyboard to be conscious of the melodic functions.

Would it not be a good idea, therefore, to let the teaching of the piano (even to professional pupils) begin with learning first to play melodies well, and after that, melodies with a simple accompaniment? In any case, it cannot be denied that with advanced pupils it is always necessary to devote special attention to the good rendering of the melody.

It will at least always be observed that those who are masters of the art of music, be they conductors, instrumentalists or singers, are masters in the rendering of melody. Such rendering has nothing artificial about it; on the contrary, by the perfect balancing of the accents within the framework of the form, it makes the melody sound so complete and natural that it is revealed as a living thing with an immediacy and inevitability like that of the wonders of nature.

In teaching, too, the practice and mastery of the art of melody in the foregoing sense can be very useful. Could not the conscious hearing of the functional laws of melody be combined with solfeggio or with training in the conscious hearing of music in general? In this case a training would be possible (it has still to be worked out) which would not only be methodical but would be a much more musical method than any we have had hitherto.

The teaching of harmony, of musical analysis and of the history of music would also derive great profit from the previous training of the pupils in the theory and practice of melody. For if they understand the melodic functions, will not pupils find it much easier to harmonise and analyse pieces of music, in addition to being able to follow the evolutionary progression of a melody? Of course such a training presumes an application to the theory of melodic function on the part of the teacher — but perhaps results might be obtained in an easier, if not even more musical, manner, although this method, too, will still have to be worked out.

For from what has been said it will be clear to the reader that a knowledge of melodic function would enable the subject of song-improvisation in the Primary School to be put on an entirely new basis. On this foundation the teacher would be able both to give methodical guidance and also to correct the pupils' exercises — though here again a practical method for pupils in the Primary School has still to be designed [13].

The Secondary School of course aims at more in its music-teaching

---

[13] Note here that one can pass immediately from the melodic games suggested on page 45 to the reading of melodies in modern notation. With the use of the so-called leaping note or by pointing to the notes such a game applying the melodic laws can be played and the reading of the notes learnt at the same time, starting with short groups. The functional laws supply the teacher with a firm basis on which he can himself construct musically justified exercises.

than the Primary School. Secondary-school pupils are initiated into the appreciation, understanding and the very experience itself of art-music (the ideal way to which is the making of music oneself). And is not the first step in this experiencing of music (regarded here from the point of view of teaching, not music-making) the experiencing of the *melody* of art-music? And is it not therefore desirable that the teacher should know the laws which the language of melody obeys?

In the following pages he will also meet with subjects, like the effect of euphony and the evolution from melody to harmony, which with musical illustrations would be of interest to pupils in the higher classes.

Finally, a provisional conclusion may be drawn about University work. Both the history of music and comparative musicology demand among other things the scientific study of melody. What has been said already in this book has shown that in this field, too, an analysis and synthesis based on the functional laws and on euphony can not only be applied with great profit but can also lead to new discoveries, as the writer can testify from his own experience.

CHAPTER THREE

EUPHONY AND ITS CONSEQUENCES

§ 1. The phenomenon of euphony in melody

Their language or dialect is a living possession of a people or group. That it is living is proved by the continued absorption of new elements and dying out of the old. That the causes of this can in the one case be identified, in the other not, in no way affects the fact of this organic evolution.

The character of a language or dialect, and its historical development, is largely dependent on the specific phonetic characteristics of the people speaking it. In the same way there are also melodic characteristics, not only in the selection and use but also in the borrowing of melodic material.

In the history of a single melody — and this is the phenomenon we shall next consider — we find both chronological and regional variations. The folksong lives, grows and changes, adapting itself to the musical idiom of different times and places.

The reason for this phenomenon lies in the euphonic peculiarities of different peoples and groups — though this is not to say that all variants in folksongs are euphonic phenomena. Peoples differ also in their characteristic rhythms and in the relation between word-stress and melodic accent in their music.

The various expressions of vocal euphony can be reduced to certain principles — and these will be discussed in relation to the melody of particular periods among related peoples.

In the centuries (from the fifth to the sixteenth) during which those who were educated in Western Europe were familiar with melodies composed in the ecclesiastical modes — a period which saw the great climax of vocal melody — the most important euphonic principles in art-song (the Gregorian melody with vocal ornamentation) were the following:

1. The degrees *fa* and *do* (the subsemitonal degrees) were, quite apart from the function of the tonic in the diatonic scale, generally regarded as points of support and repose for the melody; while *mi* and *ti* (the supersemitonal degrees) were felt by the composers of the

60

religious chants and by the singers of the ornamented Gregorian melodies as transitional degrees to *fa* and *do* respectively [1].

As we have to do here with an historical phenomenon, the proof of the justice of this claim lies not in any tests applied by us but in the testimony of mediaeval music itself. For such an historical proof one has only to study the rich treasury of mediaeval melody. Yet a reference to the following characteristics of Gregorian chant will probably suffice to enable the reader to accept the thesis here put forward.

The liturgical chant made use of many ornaments of a specially vocal nature — a short and light staccato repetition of a note (*bistropha*, *tristropha*) or broad, heavy repetitions (*bivirga*, *trivirga*); a sort of portamento glide over the transitional note between the two notes of a third (*quilisma*); a kind of trembling on a note (*trigon*), and so on. Now that the euphonic principle of the supersemitonal degrees (*mi* and *ti*) being transitional notes and the semitonal degrees (*fa* and *do*) melodic strong-points was natural to this art-song follows from the fact that figures such as the *bistropha*, *tristropha*, *bivirga*, *trivirga* and *trigon* were mainly used on the subsemitonal degree (*fa* and *do*), the *quilisma*, on the contrary, preferably on the supersemitonal degrees (*mi* and *ti*). This gives some idea of the consequences of this euphonic principle in the ornamented liturgical chant [2].

2. In the period when the liturgical chant came into being musical hearing and utterance both desired a clear tonal contrast immediately *above* and *below* the tonic, a contrast satisfied completely by the principal degrees *re* and *so* but not by *mi* and *fa*. There is even a

---

[1] It will come as a surprise to many to learn that our staff-notation with the *F*-clef and formerly the *C*-clef is a result of this euphonic phenomenon. Yet it can be demonstrated historically. Not only were the *f* and *c* lines the first forms of the staff-notation but even when this was extended to four lines they continued to be distinguished by colours, red for the *f* and yellow for the *c* line; *f* and *c* were at first the only clef-letters. Why were *f* and *c* specially chosen and not some other notes? Because, as Guido of Arezzo said, these notes are the *frequenter repercussi*, the "frequently sounded" notes; *b*, on the other hand, is *ignobilis*, "base".

The choice of the *fa* and *do* degrees as melodic supports and *soni repercussi* has misled some musicologists to draw the mistaken conclusion that Gregorian chant is essentially pentatonic.

[2] In the oldest manuscripts containing musical notation, the so-called *neumes*, additional letters were used as a rough indication of pitch. For a rise to the subsemitonal degrees, e.g. from *la* or *so* to *do*, the letter *l* was generally used (for *leva*, "rise"). Apart from this particular case a rise was usually indicated by *s* (*sursum*, "high") or *a* (*altius*, "higher"), but — and this is strange — for the same pitch *and also for the minor second* the letter *e* was used (for *aequalis*, "equal"), presumably because in the succession of notes and intervals of a melody the minor second was felt to be such a small interval, one moreover with such a close affinity with the following note, that in choosing an indication of the minor second they used the first letter of the word for equality of pitch. Cf. J. Smits van Waesberghe, *Muziekgeschiedenis der Middeleeuwen II*, pp. 498-517.

distinction to be drawn between these last two. As a tonic the *fa* degree has first claim as its dominans on the favourite degree *do*; while *mi* as tonic, on the other hand, has as its dominans the note *ti*, which in the chants is in practice unfit for use in the function of dominans. The *fa*-mode thus has only one great disadvantage, while the *mi*-mode has such serious shortcomings that it has little attraction for the composer of plainsong.

It is instructive to see what history has to say about this matter [3]. This is what we find:

A. At first composers seem to have avoided the *mi* and *fa* modes. At least it is generally accepted that the Tract chants are the oldest Gregorian melodies; as a form (but not all the melodies) the Gradual is with the Tract one of the oldest. However, Gregorian chant has tracts only in the VIIIth (*so*) and in the IInd (*re*) modes. Of the Graduals those in modes I/II and VII/VIII are older than those in modes V/VI and III/IV (this last group contains only a tenth of the total number of Graduals in the Old Roman Mass repertoire).

B. When people began to compose chants in the *mi* and *fa* modes, an attempt was made to solve the problem of the dissonances to which they gave rise.

a. The "fa"-mode

The remedy for the lack of a major second as a contrasting note of the tonic was found in a deviation to the minor third below. This appears not only from the melodies themselves but also from the cadences at the half-close and at the end.

In the melody, for example, an opening which in the Dorian mode would be:

and therefore in the Lydian mode would be:

[3] Cp. J. Handschin, *Der Toncharakter* p. 17: "Dies könnte uns wieder erinnern, dass deren Gegenstück (vom *d*) der Ton *g*, in den ältesten Zeiten einer schriftlich überlieferten abendländischen Melodik eine besondere Rolle spielte, war es doch neben dem *d* der Hauptgrunden der ältesten "gregorianischen" und Sequenzmelodien".

would in the *fa*-mode for the sake of euphony be:

as in the following Gregorian chant, the beginning of the *In splendoribus* (one of the oldest melodies in the VIth tone):

The figure used here at the melodic half-close on *utero* and *luciferum* is *FGFD*. Why? In the *re*-mode we should have *DEDC*, which in the *fa*-mode would become *FGFE*. For the sake of euphony the last note *E* deviates to *D* as a better contrasting note to *F*. This deviation has one most important result, namely that the contrasting third of *F* in turn deviates from *G-E* to *G-D*. This fact will only be mentioned now, but later it will be made clear why it is so important.

Not only, then, is *FGFD*, ending on the lower third instead of the lower second, the usual formula for the half-close in this mode, but in some other cadence-forms which make use of notes below the tonic *D-G* is substituted for *E-G* (as in the above example where, at the beginning of the final cadence, on *génui*, *D* and *G* are accented rhythmically before the appearance of the tonic *F*).

b. The "mi"-mode

The solution applied in the *mi*-mode is indicative of the preference for the subsemitonal degrees *fa* and *do*. The composers of the Gregorian chants, who bestrewed their melodies with a rich mosaic of flowing ornament, applied the principle of euphonic deviation skilfully to run a melody which was supposed to be in the *mi*-mode over into the *fa*-mode, with the result that in most of these compositions large portions, if not practically the whole, have *fa*-modality [4]. The tonic *mi* is shifted to *fa*, the dominans *ti* to *do*. Now the original reason for

---

[4] This is especially true of the plagal *mi*-mode; the authentic *mi*-melodies often pass into the plagal *so*-mode with *do* as dominans. But whether the *mi*-mode chants go over

the medians or the plagal dominans of the *mi*-mode being not *so* but *la* has been sought for years in vain, but from what has just been said the underlying cause of the phenomenon is so obvious that there is no necessity to emphasise it. Although it is true that in the course of time many original *ti*-notes were for the sake of euphony altered to *do*, the opinion which has gradually formed that *at a particular time the so and ti dominantes of the mi-mode were changed to the la and do dominantes* is incorrect. The truth is that the composers of the chants who wrote melodies in the *deuteros* or *mi*-mode in accordance with the theory that "there are four principal modes, namely on *re, mi, fa* and *so*", had no other alternative than deviation to the *fa*-tonic with *do*-dominans in the authentic mode, with the necessary consequence of the *la*-dominans in the plagal mode. But it still remains true that various parts of these chants (especially the opening and of course the concluding sections) make substantial use of a *so* and a *ti* dominans [5].

c. The "so"-mode

The *so*-mode has no defect as far as the contrasting third (*fa-la*) and the contrasting fifth (*fa-la-do*) are concerned, but its medians or plagal dominans *ti*, being a supersemitonal degree, is not very acceptable in this function. As a result, *do* becomes the deviation-note of *ti*. In the very heart of the Middle Ages (in the tenth and eleventh centuries) we find examples of *ti*-notes in the *so*-mode being changed into *do*. The manuscripts give clear proof of this. Yet it must not be concluded that *at the time of composition* of the chants it was impossible for *do* to occur as a deliberate deviation of the *ti*-degree. From the beginning the composers made use of deviation, but in the course of time this euphonic deviation was further extended in vocal practice, not only in Gregorian chant but also in folksongs.

3. Gregorian chants in the *re*-mode (Dorian) make frequent use, especially at the beginning, of a figure which is termed "modal repercussion". This consists of the tonic-dominans interval with an accentuation of the last note. In the plagal Dorian mode this figure would be *re-fa-so-fa* (see Example 26, *Dominus dixit*, on page 42); in the authentic Dorian mode it was originally sung *re-la-ti-la* (or *re-do-re-la-ti-la*). But does this sound well? The *ti* is unpleasant and is not easy to sing. About the year 1000 two variants arose. In the Germanic

into the *so, re* or, as predominantly, the *fa*-mode, the reason for all these departures is the same, namely that composing consistently in the *mi*-mode was avoided for the reasons of euphony already mentioned. In psalmody the reciting-tone (i.e. the dominans) in the authentic third-mode is *do* instead of *ti* and in the plagal fourth-mode *la* instead of *so* (see p. 99 f below).

[5] It is obvious from what has been said that in the final cadence *mi* will be avoided immediately before *fa*. Thus one gets, not G-E-F-F-E (as in other modes, e.g. F-D-E-E-D, a-F (=FGaGF)-G-G-F, b-G-a-a-G) but E-G-F-F-E, which avoids the order E-F-F-E.

lands (including North Holland and Limburg) the *ti* in this figure was altered to *do* (the so-called Germanic "dialect" of plainsong), in the Romance countries to *te* (the so-called Romance "dialect"). In many other places the Germanic dialect changed the figures *la-ti* and *re-mi* into *la-do* and *re-fa*. The subsemitonal degrees *fa* and *do* thus not only became melodic points of repose (in contrast with the super-semitonal degrees *mi* and *ti*), but in addition were also much used as *accents*. The existing melodies were altered accordingly. In the final revision of the plain chant (the *Vaticana*) the Germanic variation has practically disappeared, the Romance variants being almost exclusively adopted, as in the modal-repercussion figure in the authentic Dorian mode referred to above.

4. The augmented fourth, which was originally accepted in melodic practice, was for reasons of euphony gradually replaced by the perfect fourth by the change of *b-durum* into *b-molle* (*ti* into *te*). (In the Middle Ages not only was the *b* flattened in the sequence *D-E-F-G-a-b* but also, at least in vocal practice, the *B* an octave lower, especially when *B♭-D* was the contrasting third of *C*).

5. Although *b-molle* was adopted by the side of *b-durum* and in actual performance the *semitonium* was slipped in where it was banned by theory and notation, yet Gregorian chant is essentially diatonic. These accidentals make their appearance not as a euphonic evolution of the melody but as an effect of the influence of polyphony, which began to make itself felt after about 1100: in the Dorian mode in the transition to the tonic (e.g. *c* sharp-*d*) and at other melodically important strong-points (e.g. *g* sharp before the dominans *a*). It was the influence not of monophonic melody but of polyphony which after centuries established the principle of the leading-note and finally led to the adoption of the major and minor scales.

The difference in the order of the notes in the ascending and descending minor scale is based on the same euphonic principle [6].

---

[6] The starting-point is the minor scale on *a* (the Aeolian) without sharps (the order of the notes, both ascending and descending, being that of the so-called descending melodic minor scale). Next the seventh note *ascending* was euphonically sharpened to the leading-note (*e-f-g* sharp-*a*, the so-called harmonic or theoretical minor scale). Lastly, as a euphonic result of this, *e-f-g* sharp-*a* was changed to *e-f* sharp-*g* sharp-*a* (the so-called ascending minor scale).

If the same sequence (*a-g* sharp-*f* sharp-*e*) is heard *descending*, it does not give the impression particularly of a minor scale; it sounds major. To make it sound minor one could have *a-g* sharp-*f*-*e* (the so-called harmonic or theoretical minor scale), but this is not very good from the point of view of euphony. As in *descending* a leading-note is not necessary (as at one point in musical evolution it was ascending), the following order, justified by euphony as well as by its minor character, is to be preferred: *a-g-f-e* (the so-called descending melodic minor scale). It can be seen from this that the names "melodic" and "theoretical" are also to be explained as a result of the principle of euphony (see footnote on page 91 below).

If, then, as has been noted, the phenomena of euphony are of a temporal and regional character and if the major and minor scales are the result of euphony in the ecclesiastial modes, then it follows that these also are dependent on time and place. There is no need to be surprised, therefore, if outside Europe (and even in some parts of Europe) this concept of tonality is not found, or at the fact that the European feeling for tonality is quite capable of changing.

Here we touch upon the provinces of physics and the psychology of music. However attractive it might be to compare what can be learnt from the newly discovered laws of melodic function with the opinions of scientists on tonal progression, tone-systems, modal relations, and so on, a study of such matters must be postponed. Yet attention may be drawn in passing to certain dangerous and incorrect views current in these sciences about our tonal system and the structure of our major scale. It is too strongly stressed, for example, that "the phenomenon of the octave is the *alpha* and *omega* of the whole musical system and of musical hearing" [7], and that the Pythagorean principle according to which the notes of the C scale can all be derived from the "circle of fifths" (*F-C-G-D-A-E-B*) "dominated ancient and mediaeval music" [8]. What has been said in these chapters is sufficient to prove that the octave, if it is perhaps the *alpha* of musical hearing, is at any rate not its *omega* [9] and that mediaeval music was not dominated by the principle of the fifth. For the rest, it may be suggested to physicists and especially to psychologists that they should take into account in their investigations the melodic principle of the "chain of thirds" discussed in this book.

Detailed scientific discussions have been devoted to the connection between the "circle of fifths" and the notes of our system (*F-C-G-D-A-E-B*) — because this contains the diatonic series; because the C scale lies in the centre of the left-hand (*F-C-G*) group of "masculine notes"; because their extension upwards produces the regular series of sharps (*B-F* sharp-*C* sharp-*G* sharp-*D* sharp-*A* sharp) while extension downwards gives us the flats (*F-B* flat-*E* flat-*A* flat-*D* flat-*G* flat); and because our harmony is based on the principle of the fifth, with the progression I-IV (lower fifth) - V (upper fifth) - I as its main foundation.

But if by way of a test one selects from the series *F-C-G-D-A-E-B* not, arbitrarily, the note C and not a "strongly masculine" note (why *should* the keynote of our system and scale be "strongly masculine"?), but the note which is the *middle* one of these seven, the *centre* of both the "masculine" and "feminine" notes, the Protos or *First* of the mediaeval *toni*, namely the note *D*, then we observe in addition that this is the *only* note in the series of fifths the intervals on either side of which are placed symmetrically (*D-E* and *D-C* a major second, *D-F* and *D-B* a minor third, *D-G* and *D-A* a perfect fourth, *D-A* and *D-G* a perfect fifth, etc.). Does not, therefore, the choice of *D* as starting-point rest on a firmer basis than that of C? If now starting from *D* we take the series of *thirds D-F-a-c-e-g-b'* then we have (1) the diatonic series, (2) a regular alternation of minor and major thirds, (3) on the left the beginning of the principal thirds (*D-F-a-c*), on the right of the contrasting thirds (*c-e-g-b*), so that the melodic laws can be read from them; further, (4) these two series are the main supports of the harmony of the Middle Ages and the Renaissance (see page 77), and (5) a reversal in the alternation of the thirds (from minor-major to major-minor) gives us,

---

[7] No criticism is intended of Prof. G. Révész's *Introduction to the Psychology of Music* (London 1953), from which this quotation is taken (p. 70), in as far as the laws of melodic functions were unknown to that science.

[8] Ibid., p. 32.

[9] Mediaeval musical *theory*, being a continuation of Greek and Romano-Greek theory, does, it is true, take the octave as its starting-point, but not mediaeval *practice*, either in the teaching of singing or in its practical exercises on musical theory.

66

ascending, the series of sharps (*D-F* sharp-*a-c* sharp-*e-g* sharp-*b*), and descending the flats (*b* flat-*g-e* flat-*c-a* flat-*F-D* flat). Note that in this system the simplest consonances such as the fourth and fifth play no part but only the "imperfect" intervals, major and minor thirds. Note also (1) that (although the fifth does to some extent play a part in the series of thirds) the laws of melody are based on those of the third, and (2) that these laws were consistently applied, even if modified by euphonic principles, in both the unisonal and the polyphonic music of the Middle Ages.

To return to our starting-point, the euphonic deviations, we may now inquire into the functional effects of these. The first thing that strikes us is the double function which certain notes have as a result of deviation. *Do*, for example, can belong to the series *fa-la-do* and can also be a deviation of *ti* and thereby be related to *so*. Thus in the *fa*-mode *re* is a member of the group *re-fa-la*, but also as a deviation of *mi* (deviation from *fa-mi-fa* to *fa-re-fa* and change of *so-mi-fa* to *so-re-fa*) it can replace it in *mi-so-te* and thus belong to the group *re-so-ti*. This is called the double function of a note arising as a result of euphonic deviation (in these examples the double function of the notes *do* and *re*).

Secondly, arising from the change of the interval, there is the change in the function of the interval. This we can examine easily in the change from *D-a-b-a* to *D-a-b* flat-*a* or *D-a-c-a* (see § 3 above). In *D-a-b* flat-*a* the flattened *b* retains the function of prosodic note of *a* although this is weakened. In *D-a-c-a* the increase of the interval from *a-b* to *a-c* on the one hand is still of the nature of an accent, and on the other hand gives rise to a functional unit as with thirds, although in comparison with the usual tension between the notes of a third, this accentuation-third loses something of its force — it is an extended melodic accent which happens also to be a third, whence the term "double function".

Perhaps this may be clearer if in the sequence *FD-F-EC-DED* (close of an Introit chant in the IInd mode) the final group *DED* is altered to *DFD* (i.e. in the Germanic tradition, which would also change *EC* to *FC*).

Here, that is to say in the so-called Germanic "dialect", the prosodic note of *D*, namely *E*, is shifted to *F* in *D-F-D*. Its character of melodic accentuation of *D* remains, but the third *D-F* here has not the tension it has in, say, the *D-F-G-F* at the beginning of the *Dominus dixit* (Example 26 on page 42). The deviation therefore preserves the prosodic function but the *new interval* resulting from the change (namely from the second to third) is weakened.

If we go a step further and regard *G-D-F* as a deviation of *G-E-F*, then on the one hand *G-D* has the function of the so-called contrasting third but on the other hand this fourth consists of a combination of a second and a third. Thus in the Middle Ages the deviation of *G-b* to G-c was felt to be on the one hand an "expanded" third and on the other a third plus a second.

The euphonic deviations accordingly gave rise to deviation-*notes* with a double function and to *intervals* with a double function, such as both prosodic function and third-function (this is called a deviation-third, being the third produced by deviation from a second) or, to give another example, both third-function and fourth-function (termed a deviation-fourth, produced from a third as the result of deviation). But it is time now to turn to our own music and to ask what the position is of G-c in the modern C major scale.

To deal fully with this question we should have to anticipate the discussion of the major scale and of the melodic significance of the fourth, but a brief summary of the answer may serve as an introduction to both these topics.

The major scale represents a delimitation of the melodic functions within the compass of the octave, in that beyond the octave the functions are simply repeated, and this not merely theoretically but in a full musical sense (such limitation was not known in the mediaeval modes and hence in learning to sing no modal scales were sung from tonic to the octave above, but only typical melodies which reproduced the characteristics of the various modes). The seventh degree has the character of a leading-note, forming a melodic unit with the second above, the octave. In the Middle Ages an interval such as this would be regarded in the progression of notes and intervals as falling under the heading *aequaliter*, that is to say, *ti* (*b*) is *melodically* the same thing as *do* (*c*). Accordingly the third-series is *C-E-G-b=c*. This is based originally not on a harmonic but on a euphonic principle. If, now, to study the function of G-c we take the series *C-E-G-b-c* it will be observed that to our ear the upper octave concludes the series of thirds (in contrast with the Dorian series *D-F-a-c-d-g*). It is immediately obvious, in other words, that, compared with the Church modes, the major scale represents a curtailment of the mediaeval melodic framework, thus reducing the number of possibilities of interplay between thirds and contrasting thirds.

Of G-c it can be said that in the major scale it is so much a unit that one may well ask whether there can be any question of a latent combination G-b-c. The fourth G-c (still starting from C) is thus at the same time both a perfect fourth, that constitutes a unit, and an "expanded" third. For if one sings only *G-E-C-b* it is noted that melodically there is between *b* and *c* so small a difference and so great a unity that (melodically, not harmonically, considered) the melodic possibilities of *C-E-G-b* as *independent* degrees are exceedingly limited. The ear prefers *C-E-G-c* to *C-E-G-b*; e.g. *C-E-G-c-a* sounds better than

C-E-G-b-a. The fourth *G-c* on the dominant is a unit in virtue of its function of "expanded" third.

This cannot be said of all the fourths in this scale. When the fourth *C-F* is heard it has a dual content, consisting of either *C-E + E-F* or *C-D + D-F*; it jumps from the principal third (*C-E*) to a counternote of the principal third, namely *F*. This is therefore termed a transitional fourth, in contrast with *G-c* in C major, for this fifth *C-E-G* proceeds to *c* (*C-E-G-c*), thus remaining in a series with its starting-point. It is not a transitional fourth but is called a *quarta consonans*. In harmony the difference in character between this fourth and the other fourths in an octave has already been observed, albeit as a harmonic phenomenon; it was called the *quarta consonans* and this term can also be kept as a melodic function in the major and minor scale [10].

This is not to say that in a melody *every* fourth on the fifth (cp. *G-c* in C major) is a *quarta consonans*. In certain melodic progressions a combination is possible (although exceptional). Such a possibility *may* be latent in *G-a-G-c* (*G-a-c*) and *G-c-b-c* (*G-b-c*) or when there is a strong rhythmical stress on *G* giving it the function of a tonal centre (dominant function). But more will be said about this in the next section on the fourth.

What are the consequences of these euphonic variations as far as folksongs and the teaching of melody to-day are concerned? Let it be stated first that these changes, made for reasons of vocal euphony in existing melodies and in the laws of melodic structure, are far fewer in the *syllabic* chants. A purely Phrygian melodic composition in the *ornamented* Gregorian chant style (the so-called neumatic and melismatic chants) is of the greatest rarity — but not in the syllabic style.

For the rest, this question can be answered as follows:

1. Of Dutch and Flemish folksong melodies in the old Church modes (apart from those in the Lydian with *bb* = Ionian) by far the greater majority are in the Dorian and Mixolydian modes; a small number in the Phrygian mode.

2. In Primary Schools where improvisation in the old modes is practised and where the children's songs are related to the modes, the child seems to have a preference for the Dorian and Mixolydian modes.

3. In the old German (and therefore partly also in the Flemish and Dutch) folksong, especially in religious song, the influence of the so-called Germanic accentuation (*la-do* for *la-ti* and *re-fa* for *re-mi*) is noticeable.

4. To our ears just as to mediaeval ears the repeated use in a melody of a *minor* second (unless it has linking function) sounds

---

[10] The first to discuss the *quarta consonans*, in a harmonic context, of course, was Franchinus Gafurius, in his *Practica musicae* (1496), Book V, Chapter 4.

monotonous, on account of its lack of the characteristic contrasting function exhibited by two notes a *major* second apart. A song like *O Friesland, zo vol deugden* ("O Friesland, full of virtues") may be centuries old but it has its faults in this respect in the opening and closing sections, so that one is tempted to ask whether it really was the folksong of the region in the true sense of the word.

In the course of the centuries the European folksong was affected by the euphonic deviation-principle, especially during the period when vocal music reached its climax. From a study of its influence one can draw the following useful conclusions for the writing of melody to-day:

1. Be sparing in the use of the minor second, except where it has linking function.

2. In applying the so-called law of the contrast of thirds a *fa* or *do* degree (leaving out of consideration any demands made by the form) finds a more effective and characteristic contrast in *fa-re-so-fa* and *do-la-re-do* than in *fa-mi-so-fa* or *fa-mi-fa* and *do-ti-re-do* or *do-ti-do* respectively.

3. In composing melodies in the old Church modes a raising by a minor second is desirable of those dominans notes and accentuations of dominantes which occur on a supersemitonal (*mi* and *ti*) degree.

§ 2. The functional affinities of the fourth

In the section on euphonic deviations a distinction was made between three sorts of fourths:

1. The fourth, whether subdivided or not, with transitional function, that is, a fourth which causes the transition from the notes of the principal third to counter-notes or *vice versa*; this is termed the transitional fourth (e.g. *A-(C)D*).

70

2. The fourth with double function as a result of deviation (e.g., *c* as deviation of *G-b*); this is called the deviation fourth.

3. The fourth as a functional unit without double function though also the result of deviation (e.g. the fourth *G-c* in C major); this is the *quarta consonans*.

It follows from this subdivision that all fourths which are not affected by euphonic deviation and which are not *quartae consonantiae* give rise to functional transition: all these fourths are *a combination of a second and a third or, vice versa, a third and a second*. This is not only an immediate consequence of the laws of melodic function but it can also be tested by experiment. Do this by examining any melodies you please, whether previously existing or composed by yourself, and seeing whether there are in them any fourths having transitional function, that is to say, which start with one of the principal thirds and end in one of the contrasting notes, or *vice versa*. If such occur, then the logical conclusion is that these fourths contain a latent combination of a second and a third. Now to analyse one of these fourths into its constituent notes:

a. Examine in a melody the progressions of fourths which in broken form consist of a third and a second (or *vice versa* — it is better to begin with Gregorian melodies), by singing them undivided, that is, without the second. The ear will then more consciously observe that such fourths cause functional transition.

b. Next, examine these undivided fourths more closely. At first one will be faced by the difficult question: what *is* the latent composition of these fourths? In many cases the following indications, which give an analysis, not of all such fourths but certainly of the great majority, will be of assistance.

1. If no positive indications are present of a different composition, and if they are not *quartae consonantes*, then the following fourths generally subdivide as follows (this is especially true in plainsong):

do-fa = *do-re-fa*, but (descending) *fa-do* = *fa-mi-do*
mi-la = *mi-so-la*, but *la-mi* = *la-fa-mi*
so-do = *so-la-do*, but *do-so* = *do-ti-so*.

2. The indications of a different composition referred to in § 1 above are contained in the following law: the immediately preceding second or third, reckoned from the lowest note of a rising fourth or from the highest note of a descending fourth, indicates the composition of that fourth — e.g., the note *a* in regard to the fourth *G-c* in the groups *G-a-G-c* and *a-c-G*; or *F* in regard to the fourths *D-G* and (as a descending fourth) *a-E* in the groups *D-F-D-G* and *a-F-a-E* respectively. The preceding second or third thus indicates the composition of both ascending and descending fourths.

All this is only a matter of analysis, not of the writing of melodies.

In melodic composition the fourth is a very welcome interval on account of the possibilities it offers of functional transition. Some of the most important of these are the following:

1. Variation in the composition of *two* successive fourths on the same note, e.g. G-c-G. If we have a second plus a third (e.g. G-a-c) and a third plus a second (e.g., G-b-c), then the succession of two of these differently constituted fourths (G-a-c-b-G or G-b-c-a-G) is particularly lively in effect. Such combinations can be given in full subdivided in this way or, if not broken, can be heard as latent in the context (e.g., c-b-G-a-G or c-b-c-a-G).

2. Variation in the composition of *three* successive fourths on the same note, e.g. second + third (G-a-c), third + second (G-b-c), second + third (G-a-c). We have an example of this in the melody of *In dulci jubilo*.

The form of the sections of this melody is a-a, b-b, b'-b' (or c-c), -b, as follows:

In dulci jubilo = a
Singhet ende weset vro = a
Al onser herten wonne leit in presepio = b
Dat lichtet als die sonne in matris gremio = b

Ergo merito = c (or b' in view of the repetition on *herten wonne* and *als die sonne*)

> *Des sullen alle herten sweven in gaudio* = b.

If now we examine the melody, then section "a" is not very original — just *do-me-so*. Nor is the second section "b" (*leit in presepio*), which only gives the continuation up to the octave — *so-la-ti-do*. Yet these are the two supports of a good intermediate passage, on *Al onser herten wonne*. In *so-la-so-do* we recognise the fourth, namely *so-la-do*. It might have been repeated as *do-la-so* on *wonne*, but then everything characteristic about it would have been lost. But instead of *do-la-so* we hear first *do-ti*, the beginning of a differently constituted fourth, and immediately afterwards *do-la-so*, thus at once imparting to this song a characteristic flavour — especially after the simple beginning of the "a" section and the equally simple continuation in the "b" section; and especially, too, in that after twice repeating the "a" and "b" sections the composer exploits to the full his happy find. Twice in succession he repeats this composite fourth (*Ergo merito, ergo merito*) and then lets us hear it once again in the context of the "b" section. It is to this succession of composite fourths that the song owes its beauty.

3. The fourth as an ornament of the third. Instead of *F-D-F* one can have either *F-C-D-F* (or *F-D-C-F* or *F-C-F-D*) or *F-D-G-F*. In the first case C functions as an accent, that is, it is a prosodic note of *D*; in the second case G is prosodic note of *F*. One can see from these examples that it is not necessary for a prosodic note to come between two notes of the same pitch (*D-C-D, F-G-F*).

4. The fourth as the opening of a melody (*quarta consonans*) or of a melodic section or phrase. The introductory fourth has a long history, which can be summarised briefly as follows.

The old Gregorian chants make use of the lower fourth at the beginning of a melody, yet this is practically always a subdivided fourth. The melody generally rises or falls to the fourth through one or more intermediate notes or *via* short figures. In the late Middle Ages both the subdivided and undivided fourth occur at the beginning of folksongs and chants. The modes are still being used but the idea of the functional unit (*quarta consonans*) is growing. In the following period, which saw the triumph of the major scale, the claim of the introductory fourth to constitute a functional unit with the fundamental note was definitively settled. The functional unit of the *quarta consonans* has been discussed and explained on page 69 above; only when the first note of the introductory fourth is rhythmically accented can it have transitional function, namely dominant function (V — see page 93 below).

As introduction of a *part* (not the beginning) of a melody a fourth can give it liveliness. Thus when the principal thirds have been stressed as the most important material in what precedes (e.g. *a-c-a*), it is particularly effective if the next section begins with either (1) the upper fourth (a-d) or (2) the lower fourth (a-E) or (3) the lower fourth of the third *c* (c-G) and if after this the fourth which has been reached is chosen as the new tonal centre of the immediately following section.

A melody in which this is done is the following Dutch folksong, which occurs with several sets of words, of which the best known are *Het viel een hemelsdouwe* ("There fell a dew from heaven") and *Gegroet U Koninginne* ("All hail, O Queen majestic"):

Analysis. In the first two bars we have the principal thirds *D-F-a*; the third bar stresses the counter-third *G-E* supplemented by *F* and *D* (counter-third cadence *G-(F)E-D*). This section thus has sufficient musical contrast in itself even though its chief contribution is the confirmation of the tonic with its two principal thirds (*D-F-a-F-a*), followed by a cadence (in bars 3 and 4).

Then the composer has a happy idea, namely to make a contrast with this section by starting on the principal third *F* and descending immediately to the lower fourth (*C*), this counter-note of the fundamental *D* then being given prominence (*F/CCDD/CA*). This section began with *F*, one of the principal thirds of the tonic (*D*), after a preceding close on this; by descending to the lower fourth this *F* caused a transition to the counter-note-series (*C* and *A*). In the same way, after the close on *CA* in bar 6 follows an opening on *C* which is immediately succeeded by its counter-notes *D-F-a*. In this way we get a melody which is full of variety and yet at the same time wonderfully simple and attractive.

Exercise. To compose melodies with notes ranging from a fourth to a seventh and introducing the interval of a fourth.

Note 1. Both the subdivided and the undivided fourth can be used in a cadence. What was said on page 36 about the principal types of cadence can thus be re-stated more fully now as follows:

Contrasting-third cadence, e.g. *d-b-c-a-b-G* (fundamental note *G*), *c-a-b-G, c-a-G,* etc. (or with fundamental note *a, e-c-d-b-c-a* or *d-b-c-a-b-G-a,* etc.).

Counter-note cadence, e.g. *b-G-a-G, bb-G-F-G, G-a-G, G-F-G, a-G, F-G,* etc. (or, with fundamental note *a, c-a-b-a-, c-a-G-a, a-b-a,* etc.).

Fourth-cadence, e.g. *c-G, D-G* (the cadence with subdivided fourth is termed either contrasting-third cadence, e.g. *c-a-G, D-F-G,* or principal-third cadence, e.g. *c-b-G, D-E-G*).

Principal-third cadence, e.g. *d-b-G, d-G, b-G, d-c-b-a-G-a-b-G.*

Repetition of fundamental note, e.g. *G-G.*

There are also mixtures of these types and, as has already appeared from the examples, they can occur with all sorts of variations. It is both possible and desirable to classify melodic cadences by the names of these types.

Write cadences with the fundamental note on the first and second degrees; analyse the cadences of old folksongs.

Note 2. Here is a melody by the famous Minnesinger Neithart von Reuenthal:

The following points are worth noting:

1. In this example the Dorian mode can be heard as an octave-unit. This song represents a preliminary stage of the minor scale that existed in the mediaeval secular song. There is another type which uses the Aeolian mode.

2. If this melody is compared with the melody by the same composer given on page 55 (Example 38c) a difference will be observed in the treatment of the Dorian mode. In the latter we have a consistent use of the "chain of thirds" (*D-F-a-c-e*), while in the former (Example (45a) we have an octave-unit (*D-F-a-d*).

75

Note 3. It is not necessary to devote a special section to the sixth, which seldom occurs in vocal music while in folksong this interval is altogether out of place. When it does occur in vocal or instrumental music then it is melodically a composite of either third + fourth, fourth + third (or *quarta consonans* + third if it begins on the lower fourth), fifth + second (e.g. from tonic to dominant + prosodic note) or second + fifth (these fifths can also be subdivided into thirds). Like the fourth, therefore, the sixth (except when it contains a *quarta consonans*) can also have transitional function.

§ 3. From melody to harmony and from harmony to melody

A book on melody has no need to concern itself with harmony, still less with the historical development of European polyphony. However, in view of the fresh light thrown on these subjects by the newly discovered laws of melody, it is only right that some mention should be made of the most important points raised.

There follows, therefore, for those who are interested in the historical relationship between melody and harmony a short digression on the evolution of harmony in Europe. This evolution proceeds at first *via* the vertical expression in chords of the horizontal melodic functions of unisonal song. The treatment of this subject on the basis of the new laws of melody requires a long preliminary study which has yet to be undertaken. Still, the main lines of the historical relationship between melody and harmony and the evolution of harmony can be indicated briefly. Such a summary on the basis of the melodic laws provides:

1. An illuminating insight into the principle of harmonisation;
2. The solution of several problems relating to early methods of harmonising;
3. The proof from mediaeval harmonisations themselves that the mediaeval composers regarded melody in terms of the functional laws of tonal affinity;
4. Evidence derived from the history of polyphony that our harmonisation is an evolutionary phase depending on rules of euphony and thus is of a temporary character.

The first point can be dealt with briefly in the form of a few propositions with comment.

It is possible to compose melodies which are so absolutely and completely musical in themselves that it does violence to them if they are harmonised.

Many Gregorian melodies, with their rich ornamentation and free, flowing rhythm, are injured in their sheer intrinsic beauty by har-

76

monisation; one such is the example given on page 42 (*Dominus dixit*, Example 26). This the mediaeval composers realised, with the immediate result that, however much the art-music was religious music and the liturgical music the fountain-head of musical culture, the ornamented Gregorian chants were not performed by them in a homophonic harmonisation at the usual speed: when polyphony was applied either to syllabic chants or to the ornamented liturgical melodies, then these were always sung in a *slower tempo* (this is the "organum" of the 9th to 11th centuries). Also they sang a melismatic melody in ordinary tempo against a principal melody (*cantus firmus*) executed in a slow tempo (this is the melismatic *organum* of the 12th century).

The ornamented Gregorian chants can only maintain their method of performance and melodic force against a contrapuntal countermelody. Very few examples in this twelfth-century technique have survived; and with these account should be taken of the possibility of interpretation in a free modal rhythm.

It would be superfluous to describe all the stages in the development of polyphony between the 13th and the 14th century. What is of concern here is to show (as will be done as briefly as possible in the following pages) that it was the melodic functions which in the first centuries of polyphony were the foundation of the principles of harmony. If this can be done, then the principle of mediaeval harmonisation will have been discovered, or at least the direction indicated in which this principle and the laws resulting from it are to be found. It is obvious that such an investigation must start with a study of the harmonic functions in the conclusions of sentences and sections. It may be remarked at once that with harmonic hearing, as with melodic singing, there has also been a euphonic development.

As far as items 2-4 above are concerned, in the solving of problems of harmonisation in early polyphony the following points are of importance:

1. Why do the mediaeval composers in a cadence, in which there must be a sharp contrast of chords, not write the progression V - I, let alone I - IV - V - I?

2. The following is a frequently occurring cadence:

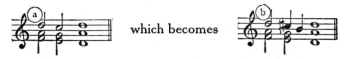

How is it to be explained that in the melodic part one generally does not find the progression *b - c♯*, which leads more smoothly to the tonic *d* than the rise of a third?

The answer to both these questions is now simple, and confirms the fact that the mediaeval composers, who long remained familiar with the plainsong repertoire, heard these liturgical chants in terms of the functional laws which have been discussed above and then applied these in their polyphonic writing. For the Gregorian cadences are based on the contrasting third or thirds of the fundamental note, namely (in the Dorian mode) on *E - C* against *D*, *G - E - C* against *F - D* or *a - D*.

The result of this in polyphony is obvious: the two-note "chord" on *C* (*C-E*) will in the cadence contrast with *D* in Dorian, *E-G* on *E* with *F* and *D*, and the triad on *C* (*C-E-G*), as well as that on *E* (*E-G-b(♭)*) with *D-a* (the third being avoided in the final chord in the Middle Ages). In this way in the polyphonic development we get in the cadences chords which, expressed in terms of degrees of the scale, can be represented by VII - I and II - I. These can also occur in the same way in the Phrygian and Mixolydian modes.

The same rule can be followed in the Lydian mode, except that here we may also have the euphonic deviation of the Lydian mode, which has already been discussed, the result becoming more graceful if, instead of *G-E* as the contrasting-third of *F*, the interval *G-D* is used or

the following progression  = VII - II - I. Here we

have two different functions before the tonic is reached. In the Dorian mode we get the same thing by altering the lower second, thus producing a leading-note (which is natural to the Lydian scale).

The fourth most important mediaeval cadence-form is II - VII - I which results naturally from the preceding. For the Lydian cadence

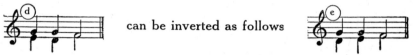 can be inverted as follows

= II - VII - I. In the same way the polyphonic Dorian cadence can be

changed from Eb-Dd to  = II - VII - I. Thus the

polyphonic cadences of the period before the application of the V - I principle can be reduced to different arrangements of two and three-note chords in the order VII - I, II - I, VII - II - I and II - VII - I.

A summary of the mediaeval cadences follows. The following are the principal points to be noted:

a. In the interests of euphony the leading-note (*sub-semitonium*) gradually comes into use, together with other euphonic alterations

78

(*colorare*). In B on the next page the two-part cadences are given first in their original form and then with a leading-note. In C the three-part cadences are given with the leading-note and other alterations in brackets.

b. Although the examples given are limited to cadences with keynote *D*, these are found also in the other modes, including those with keynotes *C* and *a*, with the appropriate alterations and with transposition (except that the VII-II-I form does not occur in the Aeolian mode)[11].

c. This historical summary gives only the harmonic chords and not the polyphonic working out of the cadences.

d. This sketch does not deal with the development to the V-I cadence-form.

e. In A are given first the most important Gregorian cadences in the *Re*-mode. The principal cadences of the *fa* (No. 7) and *so* (No. 9) modes have nothing special about them; more important is the second cadence of the *fa* mode (No. 8) because in polyphony this develops into the progression II-VII-I (or VII-II-I), which in its classical form is later used, with *musica ficta*, in the other modes (see D).

[11] In order to avoid *f♯* the Phrygian mode was transposed a fifth lower (tonic *A*).

The transposed Lydian mode has tonic *C*, the *b* being lowered to *b♭* to avoid the tritone. The introduction of alterations (*colorare*) took place at first much more frequently in unisonal than in polyphonic music, in this respect much being left to the performers themselves or rather the music often being interpreted according to personal taste, with more or less *musica falsa*.

MEDIÆVAL CADENCES

It is important now to see how the development came about from VII - I, II - I, II - VII - I and VII - II - I to V - I.

The compositions themselves prove clearly that it was a euphonic evolution which took place. In the 14th century the functional change V - I came to be recognised as a possible form of cadence, as had happened previously with the progression IV - I. That it still represented a daring experiment and not a final conviction that the definitive cadence had been found appears first from the fact that the composers who used the V - I progression continued to use the traditional cadences, and secondly from the conduct of the parts (see cadences 2 and 3 in the example below).

Thus arose the following cadences:

Development proceeded but it was more than a century before the V - I cadence-form finally triumphed, and then only as a triad. In the period 1450-1550 the progressions IV - I and V - I appear more and more frequently beside the traditional forms; beside VI - II - V - I, VI - I - V - I and I - IV - VII - I there also occurs as a possibility IV - V - I. The 17th century accepted definitively the harmonic principle of the tonic, subdominant and dominant triads, the 18th century that of the chord of the dominant seventh.

This short sketch is enough to show that the formation of the polyphonic cadences developed from the vertical writing (in chords of the horizontal (unisonal) cadences of mediaeval music, that is to say, was based originally on the melodic functional laws then in operation; and secondly, that the principle of contrasting thirds against principal thirds gradually broke down and was replaced by a new melody and harmony based on triads interchanging in the order tonic-subdominant-dominant-tonic [12].

One might consider this problem now from the standpoint that harmony should be an outcome of melody, but as we are viewing the matter historically two questions now pose themselves — first, how was the relation between melody and harmony regarded at this period

---

[12] Something should be said at this stage about the difference in the function of the fifth in melody and harmony (only the fifth *above* the tonic is here referred to).

The *melodic* function of the fifth was discussed on p. 50. There it was established that the upper fifth of the fundamental note forms a functional unit with it. Is it not, therefore, better to use for the fifth forming a unit with the fundamental note, in melodies also in the major and minor scales, the term *dominans*, which thus represents a *melodic* concept? In this way confusion and misunderstanding are avoided, for it is sometimes difficult at first for the student of music to understand why in melodies in the ecclesiastical modes we can speak of a dominant which may occur on a minor or major third, a fourth, a fifth or a sixth. The reason for this is that the term "dominant" has become too closely identified with the harmonic dominant function.

We are concerned in this section with the fifth in major and minor scale melodies, and in this connection the following should be noted.

The *dominant function* (and the same is true of the subdominant function) is one of *contrast* between the triad on the fundamental note or tonic and that with the dominant as bass-note (or with the subdominant, though we shall not refer further to this). When one talks of dominant, therefore, one naturally thinks at once of this harmonic contrasting function. Yet the dominant note can also occur melodically in a melody in a major or minor key

in the history of music (for *basso continuo*'s were written in which the other parts, including the melody, had to be improvised); and secondly, does melody lose or gain in the melodic force of its functional tensions and contrasts by reason of harmony? The answer to the first question is that harmony, harmonic life, was regarded as being of greater musical importance than melody, melodic life. The second question has already been answered above: a good melody, one not derived from harmony, has an independent life of its own, which remains practically unimpaired as long as it is accompanied by one or more other melodies, but which suffers when its notes are sounded together with chords built up on bass-notes. Hence one can say that polyphony might well have continued to develop directly from the principle of the functional laws of melody (counterpoint); then in the following centuries ever more new harmonic possibilities could have been discovered in these laws. Instead, another course was chosen: a harmony built up on bass-notes triumphed and even laid down laws for melody. Hence developed melodies which were heard harmonically, not purely melodically, melodies produced by adding together the top notes of harmonically worked-out basses, and even melodies which are either wholly or in part simply worked-out chords.

For a couple of centuries this domination of melody by harmony had its attractions but when the novelty wore off and one had to be satisfied with ever greater harmonic variety, then finally — and this is the point we have reached to-day — there are only two new ways open to us, either to advance along the road to lawlessness and chaos and let eccentricity and snobbery triumph, or to return to the point at which the wrong path was taken, to a melody restored to

forming a functional unit with the fundamental note. In these keys also, therefore, it is an advantage, in order to avoid confusion between these two functions, to use the term *dominans* when the fifth forms a functional unit with the fundamental note; for this melodic dominans is not based (like the harmonic dominant) on contrast, and by *transition* (not "modulation", for that is a harmonic concept) it can be *melodically* a shifted tonal centre — but only melodically and still maintaining its fundamental-note function. The term *dominant* is then used in the sense of the harmonic dominant when a melody is considered from the point of view of harmony or when the melody itself is thought of, as when modulation occurs, in terms of harmony. Of course it goes without saying that in general the term dominant must be used in the sense of, say, G being the dominant of C in a piece of music.

That in considering a melody harmonically several factors must be taken into account in determining whether the fifth has tonic or dominant function (especially, e.g., when the dominant falls on a beat of the bar which rhythmically is either accented or not) is a matter that concerns harmony and not melody.

This discussion will have made clear that musical terminology has for centuries been so dominated by the harmonic point of view that, if justice is once more to be done to melody, one is obliged to introduce new terms such as dominans.

82

its supremacy and a harmony derived from it, that is to say, new chords deduced from the eternal laws of the melodic functions.

This path cannot, as we have seen, consist of a new harmonisation of melodies; it can only start from the melodic hearing of melodies and from melodic composition in parts, in the direction, that is, of polyphony. Only a polyphonic or polymelodic style — in principle, at least — does no injury to the very essence of melody. Such a polyphonic style — if music were to take this new direction — would be entirely new, in as far as modern art-melody would be quite different from that of the composers of the great age of vocal polyphony. Yet this melody, despite its new rhythmical form, its new modal system, its new structure, its new alterations, and its relation to possibly new harmonic principles, would still be based on the natural foundation of the laws of melodic function, essentially independent as these are of any particular *a priori* rhythm, modality, form or euphonic alterations.

If this idea should ever be realised, then, if we entitle the polyphonic period up to about 1600 *From Melody to Harmony*, and that from 1600 to 2000 *From Bass or Harmony to Melody*, the polyphony of the future will bear the title *From Melody to Polyphony or Polymelody*.

Excursus I. Explanation of the omission in early times of the third in the final chord.

The omission of the third in the final chord before about 1600 has been discussed over and over again. Now seeing that in the present study of melody it is the paramount importance of the third which has been stressed, there is good reason for opening up this question again. The explanation would seem to lie in the concept of the final chord being different then from what it is now.

What we want now is a final chord that stresses clearly the tonality (major or minor) and mood of the work. Before 1600 composers avoided on principle what they regarded as an undesirable obtrusiveness; at the end they wanted no *chord* but the fundamental note, the tonic. Anyhow, they did not think in chords but in melodies, and a melody comes to its end on the fundamental note (see p. 44 footnote).

Three stages can be distinguished in the evolution of the final chord in European polyphony: (1) the tonic, or tonic with the octave above; (2) the admission of the fifth; (3) the general acceptance of the fifth. Why was the fifth considered admissible? After the octave the fifth has the strongest degree of consonance (Helmholtz). Then it was established experimentally that of the two-note "chords" the fifth is after the octave the last of the groups to be identified as a two-note interval (a less than 50% judgment) or, what is the same thing, as a unit with the tonic. Finally in the Middle Ages the fifth and the fourth (for the fifth divides the octave into fifth + fourth), together with the octave, were regarded as perfect consonances, and it was not until the 13th century that the third was accepted as an imperfect consonance (though here it must be remembered that by "consonance" the early theoreticians understood tonal relationship rather than chord).

Hence the fifth has a privileged position among the intervals, being, like the octave (and dividing it into fifth + fourth), "perfectly consonant" and, next after the octave, the note most strongly resembling the octave. Consequently it least disturbs the tonic character, having, in contrast with the third, a strong tonic affinitiy.

So if at the end no chord in our sense was wanted but only the tonic, then it is quite understandable that after the stage of tonic, or tonic with octave, the fifth should be regarded as admissible with the tonic and the octave, and should finally be accepted generally. Only in an entirely new evolutionary stage based on a radical change of view could the third first be admitted and then accepted. And with it the final *chord* is established.

Excursus II. Consideration of the I-IV-V-I formula.

It is now clear that the I-IV-V-I formula was also the result of a long and gradual process of evolution.

Has it also developed from melody? It has been claimed that the tonic-subdominant-dominant-tonic progression depends on a melodic functional law. Its origin has also been sought in the division of the octave into two similar fourths, e.g. *C-F* + *G-c*. Both fourths have a minor second immediately below their highest note, that is to say a note with possible leading-note function; in this view *F* (the subdominant) would have been heard as a relative ending and *G* (the dominant) as the beginning of the second fourth-series, so that the octave consists altogether of *C-F* + *G-c* = I-IV-V-I.

But however attractive to our ears is the hypothesis of a melodic foundation and however ingenious a solution the theory of the division of the octave into two similar fourths seems to be of the origin of the I-IV-V-I formula, it can be shown on historical grounds that both theories are scientifically untenable.

Anyhow, if these suppositions had any foundation in fact and if indeed they did explain the origin of the basis of our harmony, then the melodies (the major and minor melodies of later centuries as well as the mediaeval ones) would have to supply evidence of this melodic law and of this subdivision of the octave. Historically, the opposite is the case. In all the melodies of the world a cadence such as *F-G-C* in key *C* is of the very greatest rarity; this exception proves that it merely represents one of the possibilities and is not an example of an observation and consistent application of a "natural melodic law". Nor do the melodies show any greater preference for dividing the octave into two similar fourths or for a cadence based on this division. If this was not actually done in practice, one cannot admit any value in a theory based upon it. There may be some grain of truth in each of these two theories but certainly not enough to provide a complete and sufficient explanation.

Such an explanation must be justified historically — too little account is taken of this — and will only be possible when the formation of cadences in the course of the centuries can be viewed in clear historical perspective. But the preceding pages have already pointed the way to a provisional solution although it cannot be proved historically here and now. But the following is the direction in which the solution must be sought.

In the preceding section the gradual transition was stressed from the melodic to the harmonic cadence, with finally, as an admissible possibility, the V-I cadence. Its first forms (see Example 46, Nos. 2 and 3, on p. 81) were still very closely related to the melody and not yet the result of a harmony based entirely on the notes of the bass. This to our ears still vague V-I cadence becomes a new starting-point, an evolutionary phase introducing another, namely that of bass-note harmony; and there develops a new way of hearing, a listening to the bass-notes, in which the melodic contrasts are replaced by bass-note contrasts. In this new phase the V-I progression is heard as a bass-note contrast in which the "vague" melodic element of the earlier V-I cadence disappears [13]; it is the same with the IV-I contrast, which develops equally gradually into the IV-V-I contrast.

In this evolution we have the application of yet another principle, namely that of an extended cadence on the tonic (the I-IV-V-I cadence is an extended or complete cadence). As a melodic extended or compound cadence we have already met with the tonic accompanied by its lower and upper second (or *vice versa* — though of the two the first with the degrees

[13] If one were thinking harmonically one would expect that in Example 46, No 2 on page 81 the bass-note *A* would go to the tonic *D* and not to the upper fifth *a*.

VII-II-I is the stronger cadence: see page 32). We see this applied in the polyphonic period in the progressions VII-II-I and II-VII-I. Now if European polyphony had developed into a music of two-note contrasts (of thirds) built up on bass-notes, then there would have arisen a complete two-part cadence in the order VI-III-I. But what happened was a development to bass-note contrasts built up on triads, the result of which was a complete cadence in the order IV-V-I.

With this a new element was introduced into and beside melody, namely melody heard henceforward in terms of actually present or latent bass-notes (cp. the *basso continuo, basso generale*). The melody loses its supremacy, or at least has to share it with the harmony — purely melodic hearing gives place to melody heard harmonically.

One of the most striking consequences of this is that the harmony can be based on contrasting functions of the bass-notes while melodically there need be no contrasting functions at all (cf. a cadence in C major with the melodic notes *c-c-b-c*, functionally a *c*-unit, but harmonically supported by a complete cadence I-IV-V-I).

Another far-reaching consequence is that, where the *melody* might find variation in functionally equivalent notes (cf. the third-units) it is the harmony that has to seek for variety, since these notes have already been included in the first chord.

To sum up, the harmony based on the I-IV-V-I formula can be explained, not from laws of melodic function, nor from melody in general, nor from any early-discovered theoretical postulate, but directly from the development of musical hearing. It is therefore a psycho-physical phenomenon (cp. the evolution in regard to consonant chords), depending as such on a variety of influences and reactions. Already in the unisonal music of the Middle Ages we get a similar evolution which has been termed the principle of vocal euphony, that bears witness to the inner life of music. These two factors, euphony (or aural development) and the laws of melody, are the most important — though not the only — determining factors in the development of European music; they make very much clearer our understanding of the principal phases of this gradual evolution. After the period of unisonal music, in which the laws of melodic function were rigorously applied, there followed a polyphony of two kinds, one truly polyphonic, closely bound to these laws, the other homophonic, considerably less bound to them. In the next stage (the pseudo-monodic) there evolved from the existing polyphony a hearing directed to the bass-notes which led to the I-IV-V-I foundation.

The fact that in all music, as far as we can ascertain, the functional affinities of the notes of a melody are observed, together with the fact that melodies not only can be constructed but actually exist which are not improved by being harmonised or even cannot be harmonised at all, proves that these affinities are based on *laws* and therefore are of permanent application, despite the temporary supremacy of bass-note harmony. The traditional harmony, on the contrary, is based not on laws, but on rules dependent on time and place, and represents therefore only an evolutionary phase.

§ 4. The pentatonic and the twelve-note scales

The pentatonic scale which is used in their melodies by many civilised peoples is distinguished by its lack of half-tones. This is not to say that the melodies are restricted rigorously to the major second and minor third degrees. The system can best be represented by the series *Do-Re-Fa-So-La* [14]. With this material several modes or keys are possible, depending on which is the fundamental note:

[14] One can also start from *Do-Re-Mi-So-La*, which in the order of its intervals is the same as the third mode in the series given above, namely *Fa-So-La-Do-Re*. Those who still sing pentatonically make use not only of variations of pitch but also now and then of additional non-pentatonic degrees such as *Mi*, *Mib*, *Ti*, *Tib*.

I. *Do-Re-Fa-So-La*
II. *Re-Fa-So-La-Do*
III. *Fa-So-La-Do-Re*
IV. *So-La-Do-Re-Fa*
V. *La-Do-Re-Fa-So*

Further, it is possible for a melody to employ not all the notes of one of these series but, e.g., only the three lowest degrees; and it is also possible for the lower notes of the five-note series to be used below the fundamental note.

Is there any point in writing melodies using only these notes, and if so what laws and principles are to be followed?

The answer to the first question is affirmative. It is a striking fact, indeed, that in lands of European culture the children's musical interval is the *minor third* and that the typical children's song has the following scheme [15]:

The European child certainly does not hear in this any relation between the G and its lower fifth C. This melody can therefore be regarded as constructed on one or two degrees of one of the pentatonic modes (cp. mode II). In this three-note material *E-G-a a* is the prosodic note of *G* and *G* forms a functional unit with *E*.

---

[15] A derivative of this scheme is the children's song G/GGGa/GE'E/FEFG/E. There is a strikingly close resemblance between this and the song sung by the Makuschi and Wapischána women of Northern Brazil when they are grinding the manioc root:

E. M. v. Hornbostel

An indication of the depths to which the folksong has sunk, at least in Holland, is that when adults wanted to give *spontaneous* musical expression to their enthusiastic feelings for the Queen all they could do was like big children to put the words "Oranje boven, Oranje boven, leve (de) Willemien" to this children's tune. And it is not impossible that it was reminiscences of this children's song which made *Stille Nacht* so popular in the 19th century (cp. the opening bars).

Of course one could also think here in terms of a group of notes from the Dorian or Phrygian mode but historical considerations require that preference should be given to a relationship with the pentatonic scale.

If it is found, then, that the pentatonic scale is still used in children's songs, that is reason enough for composing melodies in it. And if it is asked what are the laws and principles of such melodies — rhythm and the formal relation to one another of the various parts of the melody not being considered — then reference may be made to § 1 on page 60 following. There it was noted that the composers and singers of the mediaeval liturgical chants regarded the *fa* and *do* degrees as melodic points of repose, and the *mi* and *ti* degrees, on the other hand, preferably as functional links to *fa* and *do*. Now the fact that in the pentatonic series given above *do* and *fa* are present but *mi* and *ti* are missing suggests immediately experience in the pentatonic modes [16].

Although for one reason or another a melody constructed with the five degrees of the pentatonic series may make an unsatisfactory impression, nevertheless by applying the laws given here, with corrections for the sake of vocal euphony, it is possible to compose quite a respectable melody; it is better at first to attempt this in the IInd and IVth modes. The following is an example in the IIIrd mode:

Analysis. The first two bars establish the principal third *F-a*. The figure *a-c-a* is to be felt rather as a deviation to the nearest prosodic note *c* than as a third-unit (see on page 64 f. the Germanic vocal "dialect", which alters *D-a-b* to *D-a-c*). The third bar has the cadence from counter-note *G* to *F*, *G* coming on the heavy beat of the bar by way of variation after the emphasis on the principal third in the preceding bars. The relationship *F-D* in the fourth bar is interrupted by the prosodic note *C*. In the fifth bar we again have the principal third, which calls for the linking note *G*, a welcome contrast after *FDFa*. Bar 6 requires a close on the fundamental note and could be *GEF*. But *E*, as we have seen, can be replaced by *D*; the pentatonic

---

[16] This phenomenon has even given rise, incorrectly, to the view that plainsong was based originally on the pentatonic scale (cf. Jos. Yasser, *Medieval Quartal Harmony*, New York, 1938, and H. Reichenbach, *Formenlehre der Musik*).

series chosen has no E and therefore D is necessary here as a "counter-note" of F [17]. In bars 7 and 8 we have $aFac$, interrupted by G in the functions of both transitional and prosodic note. After the principal third aF in the ninth bar, bar 10 shifts to G-E-, altered to GFD-, as in bar 6. The eleventh and twelfth bars contain a strong but ordinary cadence consisting of counter-note + principal third.

The twelve-note scale

Only a few provisional indications can be given for the application of the melodic laws to the twelve-note scale.

When in this context we speak of twelve notes, what is meant is the application of these laws and principles to twelve *independent* degrees (or some of them) and not the altered degrees of the seven-note system.

Our ear cannot (or not yet) grapple successfully with the complexity of twelve independent degrees from *do* to *ti*. A succession of five minor seconds as independent degrees already gives one a feeling of discomfort, indicating that this is a musical alphabet whose meaning escapes us. It is different with a series of three or four minor seconds. A very well known example of the first is the following Andamanese song, sung by the aborigines of the Andaman Isles north-west of Sumatra and consisting of three notes covering a diminished third. Although comparative musicology has not yet given any explanation of the functional affinities of the notes of such melodies, it is not difficult after what has been said here to analyse this melody.

M.V. Portman

The fundamental note is E, which is encompassed above and below by a minor second. According to our melodic laws what we get is that the lower and upper seconds are counter-notes accenting the fundamental note and together constituting a contrasting third against the fundamental note. Looking now at the melody, we see in the first four bars an interplay of accents, first of the upper and then of the

----

[17] This example gives an opportunity of comparing the effect of a pentatonic melody with that of one in the major scale. In F major the prosodic note c (deviation of b) in bar 2 would become bb (to avoid the tritone); in bar 6 there is a chance to use the welcome leading-note of F, namely E as a counter-note of F (thus G-E-F).

lower second with the fundamental note. In bar 5 we have a half-close on the lower second. The beginning of bar 6 emphasises the fundamental note, after which the cadence is built up: this consists of the counter-third (D♯-F), which necessitates the return of the tonic.

If primitive melodies of so few notes, of such culturally backward peoples, satisfy these melodic laws (as well as melodies throughout the centuries both in Europe and beyond) and if in general the melodies (in as far as one can call them melodies) presented to us by comparative musicology do the same, are we not justified in drawing the conclusion that these melodic laws of functional affinity are based on the natural order? This cannot be said of the harmonic functions IV-V-I, and it is for this reason that in this course principles and laws, and not merely rules, have been spoken of. And is it not also highly remarkable that this Andamanese melody should be concluded with a refrain in parts whose harmony is puzzling to us (see Example 51 below)? Yet if we examine this heterophony and analyse it vertically we see once more that we have here agreement with the mediaeval cadences which we have already seen to follow a VII-II-I formula. Does not this prove both the correctness of the melodic analysis just given and also that the principles of mediaeval polyphony are based indeed on the natural order?

The following is the present-day Andamanese refrain just referred to:

§ 5. Hints on the analysis and writing of melodies in the major and minor scales

The composition of melodies in the major scale — to restrict ourselves to this for the moment — has gradually become more and more dependent on harmonic hearing in triads and tetrachords. Already long before the triumph of the major-minor and the tonic-dominant principle use was made of alteration (especially on the seventh degree with the non-subsemitonal fundamental notes D, E, G, etc.) and with it of the principle of the leading-note with its strong urge towards the tonic. This last development, which was in origin euphonic and not harmonic, brought the melodic laws of contrasts of thirds into danger and caused the melodic functions of the seven degrees to be enclosed within the confined space of the octave.

Although the musical *theory* of the Middle Ages was familiar with the octave as a unit in the Church modes, it was unknown in the teaching of singing and nearly unknown in *melodic practice*; on the other hand it was employed frequently in the secular song — but it was the Church music which was the dominating influence. And although there has never been so much attention paid to the teaching of music in the schools as during the Middle Ages [18], yet in all the various exercises that have come down to us there are none that introduce the youthful ear to the character of a mode by means of the singing of scales. Thus the octave was not a unit in the practice of those days. It was, above all, the entry into art-music (and later into popular music) of the leading-note which made the octave a unit and the octave-note the final note of that unit. Instead of the series *D-F-a-c-e-g* and its chain of contrasting thirds *C-E-G-b-d-f* we then get *D-F-a-c♯(-D)* and as contrasting thirds *C(C♯)-E-G-b*. And with this, that is to say with the seventh degree in leading-note function, the possibilities of melodic variation become much more limited.

In addition, to an ear tuned to the tonic-dominant a number of contrasting functions are also weakened, the force of the third lying within the fifth being reduced and the functional units formed by each of the two thirds that constitute this fifth being less consciously apprehended. Harmonic hearing in triads extends this weakening of the third-units to all triads, so that what with this development and the enriching of our ear by harmony a heavy price is paid in *melodic* variation and above all in the true understanding of melody.

It is true that mediaeval monophony was familiar with the principle of the fifth-unit, but that did not imply any relationship between the tonic triad and the dominant triad. This is proved by the fact that not only was there no objection felt to turning this fifth into a sixth for the sake of euphony but also the plagal modes had as dominans a minor and a major third and even a fourth. In the way in which it was applied the mediaeval system proves itself to be based in the first place on thirds, in the second place on the combination of two thirds into a fifth, and only in the third place on the *unit* of the fifth, and even then not on any contrast between the fundamental note and its upper fifth (the dominant function in the harmonic sense).

[18] See J. Smits van Waesberghe, *School en Muziek in de Middeleeuwen*, Amsterdam, 1949. Octave-linking was often employed in the Gallican liturgical chant (see page 92), but in the old Roman Gregorian chant it is exceptional in the extreme (it occurs, e.g., in the *Haec Dies ... Confitemini* and *Alleluia, Pascha nostrum* on Easter Sunday).

The difference between the mediaeval and the later conception of melody can be summed up in three main points:

1. Instead of eight modalities we get only two, the major and the minor;

2. Instead of two series of thirds (e.g. *D-F-a-c-e-g*, etc., and *C-E-G-b-d-f*, etc.) between which there is a melodic interplay of third-units and contrasting functions, we get a small limited number of triad-units which in essence have only two main contrasts with the tonic, namely the subdominant and dominant triads;

3. Instead of the supremacy of melody we get a marriage between melody and harmony, and finally a IV-V-I harmony at the expense of the individuality of the melody — the melody comes to be heard harmonically.

It is remarkable how slowly and gradually such a radical change, for the sake of euphony (though laziness also played an important part), took place. Of the three points just mentioned it was the triumph of the major and minor which was the first to be definitely completed. (It is better to consider these, not, as is often maintained, as new keys side by side with the old [19] but as euphonic derivations from the old, the major from the Lydian and Mixolydian, the minor from the Dorian and Phrygian modes. This can be proved historically and can also be deduced from what has been said here on the evolution of the euphonic deviations) [20].

It has also been demonstrated that a centuries-long engagement preceded the marriage of melody to the IV-V-I harmony, the melodic triad-principle being the transitional factor. The major and minor keys were then accepted as the most important modes. From the point of view of melody this must be regretted, but for the time being at least it must be accepted. And with this we get harmonic functions that cut acros the purely melodic laws. One result of this is that on account of an actual or latent harmonisation a note comes to have a function different from what would be expected from the purely melodic point of view.

---

[19] This is not to deny that the *popular music* of the Middle Ages had a predilection for octave-series at a stage anticipatory of our major and minor scales; nor the possibility that these keys existed in monophonic secular music before their use in polyphonic art-music. In connection with this see Note 2 and the example on page 75 (Example 45a).

[20] Already at the beginning of the 11th century Guido of Arezzo pronounced the *bb* to be legitimate in order to avoid the tritone, and the leading-note begins to be introduced in the 12th century. To convince oneself of this one has only to sing the notes of the four principal modes with *bb* in the Dorian and Lydian and with a leading-note where this is absent, and our two scales (together with the difference between the ascending and descending melodic minor and also the harmonic minor scale) will be recognised easily in the Church modes. See also page 65, footnote.

Is it therefore necessary to have a knowledge of harmony in order to understand melodies in the major and minor keys? In one respect yes, in another no. It is necessary to distinguish here between harmonising, composing and analysing this sort of melody.

That in order to be able to *harmonise* a melody one must understand the technique of harmony is obvious, but to this it should be added that *the harmony must derive from the melody.*

In order to *compose* melodies it is not necessary to have any knowledge of harmony. The theory of melody set out here is sufficient for this purpose; as far as possible apply the laws of the third-units, of the contrast between principal thirds and contrasting thirds, of accentuation by means of prosodic notes and of euphonic deviation. And remember that the melodic functions are limited by the upper octave of the fundamental note. As a result of this limitation the octave can be divided — as was already done in the mediaeval Gallican chants — into its root triad + a fourth, i.e. *C-E-G* + *G-a-c*; one can also make use of the contrast between two subdivisions of the octave, one ascending, the other descending (occurring, among other places, in folksongs in Malacca): *C-E-G-b*($b\flat$ in Malacca)*-c-a-F-C.* Much can be done with these two subdivisions of the octave.

If one wants to go further — as is desirable and requires little effort — then one should keep an eye in addition on the most important of the harmonic functions, which are illustrated below.

Finally, the *analysing* of melodies in the major and minor keys will present difficulties, understandably, to those who know no harmony.

These difficulties will now be considered, in order that those who are not proficient in harmony may be enabled to analyse melodies of this type. This can be done by indicating merely the principal harmonic functions, in as far as they have penetrated into the melody [21].

Let us take the Christmas carol *O Herders laet Uw bokskens en schaepkens* ("O shepherds, leave your sheep and goats"). This melody, of an instrumental rather than vocal type, consists very largely of a series of broken chords and therefore is particularly suitable for this purpose — *not* as a model song melody (see Ex. 52).

The first seven bars can be analysed without difficulty according to the melodic laws given here. Bar 8, however, may give trouble.

[21] What follows here, up to page 95, is therefore addressed to this particular group of readers.

The fifth above the fundamental note forms a functional unit with it. One would therefore expect in this example that the second *c* of bar 8 (the fifth above the fundamental note *F*) would form a functional unit with *F* (and again in bar 12). But this is clearly not the case; melodically this *c* is obviously part of the third-series *C E G* which has just been heard. Thus melodically we have here a transition (see page 52) from the fundamental note *F* to a new tonal centre *c*.

This transition to the upper fifth or lower fourth of the fundamental note has under the influence of the harmonic function come to have such an importance in the major and minor keys that special attention must be paid to it [22].

The following is a brief explanation of harmonic function as it occurs in a melody.

1. First and foremost, the function of the melodic fundamental note is exactly the same as that of the tonic in harmony. The fundamental note *C* of a melody in the major has as its harmonic bass-note the tonic *C*. The triad included in the tonic function is thus *C E G*. Both the fundamental note and the tonic triad are points of repose which bring the working of the functions to a complete stop.

2. It is quite otherwise with the contrasting function.

As long as it was left to itself, melody had a number of principal-third functions on the fundamental note and a number of contrasting functions of contrasting notes against a number of principal thirds. Harmony, however, has only one tonic function and all contrasting functions are reduced to *two* main types. One of these is the dominant triad (upper fifth or lower fourth of the tonic), i.e. with tonic *C*, dominant *G* and triad *G b d*. The other is the subdominant triad (upper fourth or lower fifth of the tonic), i.e. with tonic *C*, subdominant *F* and triad *F a c*.

[22] This phenomenon is not restricted only to the music with which we are familiar but occurs also among peoples who have a totally different musical idiom. Below (Example 54) is the melody of a two-part song from Malacca (Semai) the analysis of which may be left

3. The three principal harmonies are thus (with C as tonic):

tonic triad: C E G, indicated by I
dominant triad: G b d, indicated by V
subdominant triad: F a c, indicated by IV.

Note that the tonic and dominant triads have G in common, the tonic and subdominant triads C.

4. If now the G is preceded or accompanied by notes from the dominant triad, especially if these fall on rhythmically important beats, then it assumes the function of the harmony thus suggested. The G is then said to have dominant function, rather than, as in melody, contrasting function. This was the case in bars 8 and 12 of the Christmas carol quoted above. In this the tonic is F, the dominant c and the dominant triad c e g; the c in question is so evidently preceded by notes of this chord that it exchanges its fundamental-note function for that of the dominant.

5. The same thing can happen to the fundamental note itself, which as we have just seen is a member of both the tonic and the subdominant triad. If in the melody the notes of the subdominant triad are strongly stressed, then even the fundamental note loses its true function and is included in the subdominant function. We get an example of this in the well-known melody (quoted here as an obvious specimen and *not* as a model of what a melody should be!):

C is the tonic, F the subdominant, and the subdominant triad F a c. The C in the third bar is part of a complete broken subdominant triad (though in a different order, namely

to the reader. But note the change of function of the G's, as well as the canon-like nature of the piece.

M Kolinsky

C F a) and thus it loses its fundamental-note character and assumes subdominant function.

6. In the purely melodic the contrasting function is bound up with the step of a second. In harmony, as we have just seen in § 2 above, the contrasts are brought about by leaps of a fifth in an actual or latent bass. The leap to a fifth below the fundamental note gives us the subdominant function. And from a bass-note reached in this way a further leap of a fifth can be made. In the Christmas carol already quoted the tonic, as has been said, is *F*. The leap of a fifth from the latent bass-note to *c* above introduces the dominant function, as in bars 8 and 12. From this *c* the bass can again jump to a fifth above (or a fifth beneath), thus to *G*, as happens in bar 25. By the alteration of *bb* to *b* the triad on *G* is given a pure dominant relationship to the triad on the bass-note *c*, to such an extent, indeed, that for a moment *c* seems to be the fundamental note; and it is for this reason that at the end of bar 26 we get this *c* again, serving, like a new tonic, as a point of repose. Such a change of tonic function is termed *modulation*. It is intelligible in terms of bass-notes, that is of harmony [23]. One must know something about it in order to be able to analyse our present-day melodies. A return is made to the original tonic by restoring the previous relationships, in this case by returning to the tonic triad on *F* (bar 27) and by the re-introduction of *bb* (bar 29).

7. Changes of function in the fundamental note and the upper fifth of the kind described in §§ 4 and 5, and even modulations, can also be brought about through the harmonisation of an accompaniment without the melody itself, as a melody (thus sung without any accompaniment), having any need for them. It is generally, in fact, the harmony that requires them (the principle of variety in music applied to harmony). Melody can secure such variety by alternating the two poles of a functional unit, but this is often harmonically insufficient in that the most important of these melodic poles has already been heard simultaneously below the first note. Thus harmonic variety is sought by forcing different functions upon the notes of the melody [24].

8. Our harmonically-trained ear demands, especially at the end of a composition, the IV, V and I functions, preferably in this order. In explaining the melodic functions, this must be taken into account. In a progression such as *e/dccb/c* the *dc* of the first bar must often be regarded as a subdominant and the following *cb* as a dominant function. The melody itself, however, has little need to be explained in this way.

9. Below is a table of the triads on each degree of the scale, with their harmonic functions. From this one can deduce what harmonic functions *all* the notes of the triads in the major and minor keys can have. It is simplest to illustrate this from the key of *C*.

I	*c e g*	tonic
II	*d f a*	substitute for the subdominant
III	*e g b*	substitute for the tonic or dominant — this is decided by what precedes or follows
IV	*f a c*	subdominant
V	*g b d*	dominant
VI	*a c e*	substitute for tonic or subdominant
VII	*b d f*	substitute for the dominant.

To return now to the *composing* of melodies in the major and minor keys, it may be observed that those who have not studied harmony

[23] This kind of dominant modulation also occurs in melody *as* melody, but in the history of music generally it is a consequence of the principle of harmonic modulation: its appearance in melody depends on the harmonic principle. See page 81, footnote.

[24] Thus on the third beat of bar 8 (the note *c*) one would be inclined to use the tonic triad (*F-a-c*) because the preceding bars 5, 6 and 7 (with dominant function) and the following bars (also with dominant function) call for a change of harmonic function in the interests of variety.

will find the preceding notes very useful. And in connection with this some harmful and objectionable results of the influence of harmony may be pointed out, so that they may be avoided in composition.

a. One should avoid the use of broken triads and especially tetrachords in melodies in slow tempo (e.g. *C-E-G-Bb*, which, if *C* is the dominant, is the chord of the dominant seventh in *F*). The debased folksong is to be recognised among other things by this melodic use of sentimental, drawling chords of the seventh. A good song in quick tempo can manage a sung triad but rarely a tetrachord.

b. Avoid, too, a middle section in the (sub)dominant key resembling the Trio in a March and thus constituting a restful inter-mezzo in contrast with the vigorous first section. A good melody *can* be composed on this plan but generally the result seems calculated and mannered, and it is forgotten that an effective melody is much better without any such convention.

For the sake of completeness it should be pointed out that what has been condemned in *a* and *b* above in regard to vocal melodies does not apply in the same measure to instrumental music. In quick passages broken chords, even repeated, can be instrumentally appropriate, supplying as they do a moving harmony, an effect which can be imitated by the coloratura soprano, but which in general is alien to the character of the human voice.

As a result of the considerable reduction in the number of possibilities of variation compared with those of the Church modes (especially the Dorian and Phrygian) and as a result of the confining strait-jacket of the octave and of the functions of the I-IV-V-I triads, *it is much more difficult to compose a good melody in the major or minor keys than in the Church modes.*

For this reason it is best to learn to write melodies first, if not in the pentatonic scale, then in the mediaeval modes, and only later should attempts be made in the major and minor keys.

It is to be regretted, let it be said in conclusion, that in composing and analysing melodies in the major and minor keys the laws of melody here set forth can only be used with the addition of the notes on the principal harmonic functions given above. The blame for this must fall, not on the melodic laws, but on the tyranny of harmony.

May this little book on melody help to break down the harmonic despotism!

APPENDIX

ON PSALMODY AND THE LAWS OF TONAL AFFINITY

By psalmody is meant a special way of reciting psalms, one which starts with a rise or intonation (*initium*), is varied by an internal cadence or mediation (*mediatio*) and finally ends with a fall or ending (*terminatio*). These figures occur on only a few syllables of the verse; most of the text is recited on a single reciting-tone or *tenor*. It does not follow merely from the fact that this recitation opens with an ascending figure and closes with a descending figure that the laws of tonal affinity automatically apply. Is there here any relationship to a lower fundamental note?

There are in psalmody eight main types of melody corresponding to the eight ecclesiastical modes, the tenor being determined by the dominans (later fixed as follows: I=*a*, II=*F*, III=*c*, IV=*a*, V=*c*, VI=*a*, VII=*d*, VIII=*c*). So far only the relationship between the tenor and tonic of the Church mode has been noted. Little attention has so far been paid to the tonal relationships of the three figures referred to above, and it is important, therefore, that these should be further considered.

To begin with, it should be mentioned that psalm-singing was at first extempore, and then at a certain period a number of psalm melodies were composed to suit the various Church modes. Even this was done extempore. Certain of these forms eventually gained wider currency than others, and the psalmody of the present-day Catholic liturgy has a fixed and in early times very widespread series of eight psalm-tones which were in general use at least by the tenth century. Each has a simple and a festive form, in addition to fixed rules for the placing of the syllables on the notes, as well as for melodic variations in the final cadences [1].

This prescribed psalmody thus represents, it is true, the way in which for centuries the psalms were widely sung but at the same time the way in which this singing had developed at a particular period. What this historical development was will always remain a mystery,

---

[1] The cadence variations are only partially considered here, as a full treatment would require more space than the subject warrants in this context.

but the melodic laws at least enable us to establish what the starting-point was. But whether this starting-point was a merely theoretical one or was both theoretical and practical must be left undecided.

Psalmody is based in its essential structure both on the functional unit of the third and on the principle of vocal euphony, and it is worth while to examine this relationship, which has not hitherto been noticed. It is based, then, on the law of the *functional unit of the third*: it begins (theoretically) with a rise from the opening note to the third above, which is the reciting-tone; in the four authentic modes this rise is from the upper third of the tonic to the upper fifth, in the four plagal modes from the tonic to the upper third. The reciting-tone is interrupted by the *mediatio*, beginning with an accent on the upper second and passing into a contrasting-third cadence of the tenor. About the *terminatio* all that need be said is that, many exceptions apart, it descends with variations to the tonic.

The principle of vocal euphony has caused the theoretical application of the laws of the third to be modified, that is to say, has brought about an evolution of the prescribed forms mentioned.

Let us examine now in succession the intonation and mediation of each of the eight tones or modes in each of the three following melodic forms: 1. the original (theoretical) form, 2. the present-day simple form, and 3. the so-called ornamented (Introit) form, in the last two explaining, as far as is desirable, the application of the principle of euphony.

I. The first mode, Dorian authentic:

The combining of the G-a is only an ornament; about b, the accenting or prosodic note in the authentic Dorian mode, it has already been noted (page 64 f.) that the Romance "dialect" replaced it by bb, the Germanic "dialect" by c. The Romance version has been chosen here.

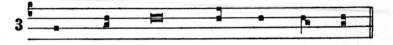

98

Here the Germanic version of the accent has been chosen and the final figure G-*a* altered to the ornamented *aG-Ga*.

II. The second mode, Dorian plagal:

Terminatio

The simple form in this mode has no real mediation, this consisting merely of an accent. The explanation is that in this way the unpleasant-sounding *E F* is avoided. For the same reason of euphony the intonation *D E F* is altered to *C D F*. Using the lower second *C* to establish the *D*, a shortened form *C D F* has been substituted for *D C D F*.
Compare with this the ornamented form:

Here there is a mediation, and use is made of the counter-notes *G* and *E*, though the *E* is used as an unimportant ornament in the figure *F E F*; only the *G* is accented.

III. The third mode, Phrygian authentic.

For reasons of euphony (*b*, undesirable as a reciting-note, being changed to *c*) the original melody becomes:

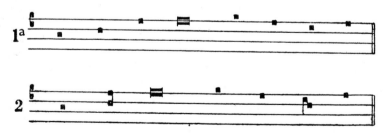

That the tenor should be shifted from *b* to *c* is easy to understand, as well as the result of doing this, namely the raising of the accenting note. In the descent of the mediation the transition *b c* is also avoided, the *b* being linked with the substitute for the lower minor second, namely *a*, producing *ba-c* (cf. what has been said on page 63 about the replacing of *GEF* by *GDF*).

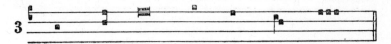

The intonation of the second section (not quoted here) is *bGac*, the ending *cb aG a b Ga*. Here the law of counter-thirds produces remarkable results: the shifting of the tenor to *c* makes the original principal third *Gb a* counter-third to the new principal third *ac* which is the result of euphonic alteration. At the end there is a strong ornamented counter-third cadence. This euphonic shift is also the reason for even the true tonic not occurring again.

IV. The fourth mode, Phrygian plagal:

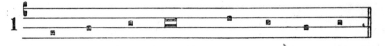

For reasons of euphony (see page 63) the original melody becomes:

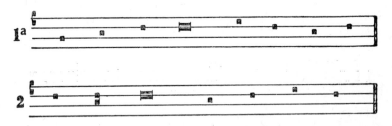

Instead of the *F G* intonation, another form must be chosen to avoid identity with the sixth mode. The starting-point, therefore, is not the tonic *F* of the sixth mode but the altered tenor-note *a*, thus removing any impression that might otherwise be given of *F* being the tonic. It is very probable that the form of the mediation was altered to conform with this unusual intonation (*a Ga*) from *b a G a* to *G a b a*.

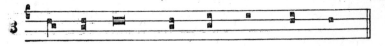

The ending, *a GF Ga G E*, is to be converted to *a GFa G E*, in which *G* is accented and *G-a* has the function of a non-accented counter-third.

V. The fifth mode, Lydian authentic:

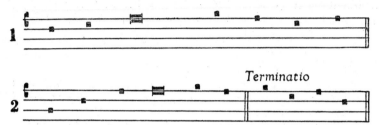

For reasons of euphony the intonation *a b c* was not welcome. The figure *G a c* would be possible but *F a c* is preferable on account of the accent on the tonic *F* and in order to avoid similarity to the intonation of the second mode (*C-D-F*). The mediation is here reduced to the accent.

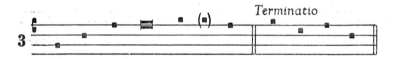

What is striking is that for reasons of euphony (i.e. to avoid the unpleasant *bc*) there is no ornamentation here, while in order to avoid the tritone the tonic does not occur at the end.

VI. The sixth mode, Lydian plagal:

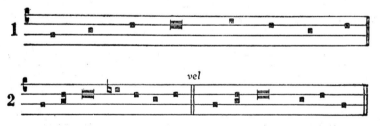

For reasons of euphony (the tritone) *b* is altered to *b♭*.

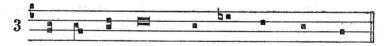

101

The final note *a* of the mediation (see 1 and 2) has here made way for the tonic *F*, not because it was necessary in this figure but on account of the evolution of the structure of the whole. For the second section of this psalm-tone has as prosodic note instead of *b* not *bb* but *c*, and this gives rise to a construction in two almost independent parts (whence the ending of the first part on *F*). The second part is the more striking of the two by reason of its higher prosodic note (cp. 3a with 3 above).

After the accentuation *a-c* the counter-note of the tonic is stressed (*G*). The ending is remarkable in that, to avoid *E* for reasons of euphony, it nevertheless chooses *D*, which gives rise to the cadence *FD F G F*.

VII. The seventh mode, Mixolydian authentic:

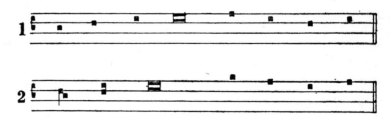

The intonation *b c* is for reasons of euphony altered to *cb cd d*. The *e*, being a supersemitonal degree, is not very suitable as prosodic note, and is changed to *f*, which makes the cadence of the mediation *f e d e*.

This is only an ornamentation of 2. The cadence of the second verse thus consists of a stressed counter-third *c-a* after the tenor on *d*, that is to say *d c a g*.

102

VIII. The eighth mode, Mixolydian plagal:

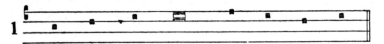

Modified euphonically this becomes:

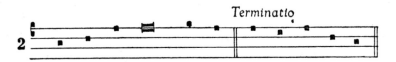

For reasons easy to understand, the tenor *b* is altered to *c*, which results in a changing of the prosodic note. In the *terminatio* the function of the counter-note *b* of the tenor *c* in the progression *c b c* is very weak. In this ending the third *c-a* occurs as a contrasting third of *G*, but as in this psalm-tone *c* is heard as the reciting-tone, it is the note *a* particularly that provides the element of contrast essential in a cadence.

In the *terminatio* here we find the opposite of what happened in 2. The notes *b* and *G* follow here in immediate succession, the third *b-G* thus becoming functionally important. It offers an opportunity for the third-figure *a-c-a* to follow, that is to say the contrasting third of *b-G* and hence also of the tonic *G*. In contrast with 2, therefore, the contrasting function in the cadence can here be expressed by *both* the notes *c* and *a*. Thus we get the formula *cbG-a-c-a-G*, which, ornamented, produces the final form *cb-Ga-cb-a-G*.

CONCLUSION

After this analysis it is impossible to refrain from calling attention to the striking confirmation of the melodic laws and the principles of euphony provided by the psalm-tones just described.

The starting-point of psalmody is an established scheme which was transposed into the various modes. These schemes were so altered by improvisation in accordance with the taste of the people of the Middle Ages, whose ears were highly sensitive to melody, that at last their original forms were no longer recognisable. Even the fundamental note and the medians and dominans suffered change.

Hitherto musicologists have been content simply to state these irregularities. But the laws of melody *explain* them. If, starting from the original scheme, one were to design a psalmody in the eight modes following these laws and the principle of euphony what one would produce would not be very different from the psalmody which has actually been established historically. This is proof that in the melodic period of music these laws were listened to even if they had not been formulated [2].

If on the basis of the laws of melody and of the principle of euphony one analyses the melodies which have come down to us from time immemorial, the melodies of the Greeks, of the Jews and of the Syrians, the syllabic and melismatic Gregorian chants, the mediaeval secular and religious song, the music of primitive peoples and of civilised peoples in all parts of the world, one will come to the same striking conclusion, namely that in all these melodies the melodic laws are applied.

By means of these laws one will be able to find the explanation that has been sought so long of the functional structure of the notes of these melodies and the same conclusion will be reached as in the analysis of the psalm-tones but on a far wider scale, namely that through all the centuries, all over the world, whatever their state of civilisation, men have listened to these laws. The proof of this does not lie within the compass of a book like the present but, in anticipation of the results of an investigation by the experts in comparative musicology, one can already carry out tests on the musical examples with which this science has already provided us. And it will be noted then that the most difficult melodies to analyse are . . . . our own, in the major and minor keys, because we have wandered far from pure melodic hearing.

---

[2] As far as is known, no mediaeval book on music gives an account of the laws of the functional relationships between the notes of a melody. That they were not formulated in the centuries that followed is only to be expected. It was the comparative analysis of melodies dating from before 1600 that led the present writer to the discovery of these laws.

GLOSSARY OF TECHNICAL TERMS

Affinity	Relation(ship), connection.
Central note	The note which assumes temporarily the functions of the fundamental note.
Contrasting fifth	The fifth which contrasts functionally with one or both notes of the principal fifth.
Contrasting third	The third which contrasts functionally with one or both notes of the principal thirds.
Contrast of fifths	The functional contrast between the principal fifth and the contrasting fifth.
Contrast of thirds	The functional contrast between two different thirds, e.g. between the principal third and the contrasting third.
Counter-note	The second which has a contrasting function.
Deviation	The alteration of a note to the second above or below for the sake of euphony.
Deviation-fourth	The fourth which has a double function as the result of deviation from a third.
Deviation-note	The note which is the result of the process of deviation.
Dominans	The dominant of an ecclesiastical mode.
Double function	a. Of a note: a note can have both its own normal function and, if it is the result of deviation, the function of the original unaltered degree.
	b. Of an interval: the two functions which arise as the result of deviation, namely the original function of the interval and the new one; e.g., of a third, both prosodic function and that of a third; of a fourth, the functions of both third and fourth.
Ending (*terminatio*)	The notes which form the final descending formula of the verses in psalmody.
Euphony	The quality of being pleasant-sounding and easy to sing.
Finalis	In psalmody the tone-ending, *terminatio* (*q.v.*).
Function	A certain mutual interaction between notes which gives rise to a relationship between them.
Functional contrast	Absolute functional opposition; it occurs with counter-notes, prosodic notes, contrasting thirds, contrasting fifths and certain fourths and sixths.
Functional identity	The absence of any difference of function, e.g. when a note is repeated.
Functional linking	The joining together of two notes which form a functional unit; thus the note which joins the two notes of a third (e.g. *so* between *fa* and *la*) has linking function.
Functional transition	The passing from a functional unit to a unit that contrasts with it (*see* transitional fourth).

105

Functional unit	The unit formed by two notes so related that the one is attracted towards the other, not by reason of any opposition between them but on account of this relationship; when the second note has been reached a tension is set up, which is relaxed on a return to the first note. This relationship is present in thirds and fifths, and in certain cases in fourths and sixths.
Function of the fundamental note	The relationship between the fundamental (or the central) note and other notes, especially those of the principal-third series.
Fundamental note	The melodic tonic. If in a melody the tonic is temporarily displaced, this new note is called the central note; the original tonic continues to be called the fundamental note.
Intonation (*initium*)	The notes which form the rising introductory formula of the first half-verse of a psalm in psalmody; sometimes occurring also at the beginning of the second half-verse.
Lower prosodic note	The second below a dominating note that functions as its prosodic note (or for the sake of euphony the minor third below).
Medians	The mediant of an ecclesiastical mode.
Mediation (*mediatio*)	The cadence at the end of the first half-verse in psalmody.
Melodic technique	The process involved in the composition of a melody.
Principal notes	The notes of a melody which are functionally important. These are obtained by omitting the notes which have functional identity and linking, the rhythmically unimportant prosodic notes and the ornaments [1].
Principal fifth	The fundamental note with the fifth above it.
Principal third	The fundamental note with the series of thirds above or below it.
Prosodic note	A melodic accent: the note which is a departure from the dominating note for the sake of stressing the latter, independently of rhythm, dynamics or word-stress.
Quarta consonans	The fourth which is a unit not involving any change of function; e.g. an opening fourth, from lower fourth to tonic.
Recitation technique	The technique of reciting on a single note (without *initium* or *finalis*) with one or several variations of pitch.
Reciting-tone	The note on which a chant is recited.
Subdivision	The division of an interval into its most important functional constituents; e.g.: subdivided fourth = third + second; subdivided fifth = third + second; subdivided sixth = third + fourth, or fifth + second.
Subsemitonal note	A degree of the diatonic scale having a semitone below it (e.g. C - BC).

---

[1] Occasionally the singular "principal note" is used to indicate one of the notes of the principal thirds.

106

Supersemitonal note	A degree of the diatonic scale having a semitone above it (e.g. *E - EF*).
Terminatio	*see* Ending.
Transition	Melodic transposition, corresponding to modulation in harmony.
Transitional fourth	The fourth which leads from one functional unit to another; e.g. *C-E-F* (i.e. from functional unit *C-E* to functional unit *F-a* or *D-F*).
Tritone	The step from the fourth to the seventh degree of a diatonic scale (e.g., from *F* to *b* in *C* major). It is the interval of an augmented fourth, containing three whole tones.
Upper prosodic note	The second above a dominating note that functions as its prosodic note (or for the sake of euphony the minor third above).
Vocally euphonious	Pleasant to hear and easy to sing.